The Turnbull Report, Internal Control and Risk Management: The Developing Role of Internal Audit

Michael Page
University of Portsmouth

Laura F Spira
Oxford Brookes University

Published by
The Institute of Chartered Accountants of Scotland

First Published 2004
The Institute of Chartered Accountants of Scotland

© 2004
ISBN 1-904574-05-X

Printed and bound in Great Britain
by Antony Rowe Ltd

RESEARCH REPORTS
REFEREEING PROCESS

The Research Committee applies a rigorous refereeing process to all stages of its research reports. The refereeing process operates by sending the initial research proposal to two independent referees (one academic and one practitioner). The academic referee will either be a member of the Panel listed below or an *ad hoc* referee. All proposals are also reviewed by the Director of Research who remains in close contact with the project. The two referees are consulted on the academic and technical standard of the draft research report. In particular, they are asked to comment on:

- the academic rigour of the document;
- the validity of the approach taken in the report;
- whether the presentation of the report identifies the key issues and brings these to the attention of the intended reader; and
- whether the document will add to the knowledge and understanding of the interested reader.

PANEL OF ACADEMIC REVIEWERS

Professor J Bebbington	University of Aberdeen
Professor V Beattie	University of Glasgow
Professor J Broadbent	Royal Holloway, University of London
Professor J Haslam	Heriot-Watt University
Professor J Holland	University of Glasgow
Professor W M McInnes	University of Stirling
Professor C Mallin	University of Birmingham
Professor H Mellett	Cardiff University
Professor M J Page	University of Portsmouth
Professor C Roberts	University of Aberdeen
Professor M J Sherer	University of Essex
Professor P Weetman	University of Strathclyde
Professor R M S Wilson	University of Loughborough

The Research Committee is grateful to all those who participate in the refereeing process.

100509795

658.

458

TUR

CONTENTS

FOREWORD

This research is interesting because it not only shows the evolution of internal audit in recent years, but also shows how it has been influenced (and continues to be influenced) by the changes that the significant emphasis on Corporate Governance have brought. The Turnbull Report was the end point of a process that originated from a requirement in the Cadbury Code of Best Practice Report calling for listed companies to report on the effectiveness of their systems of internal financial control. It was a controversial recommendation because neither company management nor auditors had been willing to take responsibility for expressing opinions about the effectiveness of a company's internal controls. However, the Turnbull Report tackled the problem in an innovative way by requiring companies to report whether the board had reviewed the system of internal control and risk management and it then encouraged them to express an opinion on the effectiveness of their systems. This linking of internal control and risk management followed similar developments in the US and Canada.

At about the same time as the Cadbury and later Turnbull Reports were being produced, the Institute of Internal Auditors had been trying to further professionalise the work of internal auditors by drawing up more demanding standards for work, improving education and training, and generally attempting to enhance the status of internal auditors in the business community. The Institute recognised the opportunity created by the Cadbury report and grasped it, and as a result was able to capitalise on the Cadbury and Turnbull recommendations. The recent Higgs report has taken things further still and it will be interesting to anticipate a further study in a few years time looking at how much further the developments discussed in this report have extended.

The research report was based on a number of wide-ranging interviews with senior internal auditors in large UK businesses, covering a range of industry sectors. The interviews covered themes such as Turnbull and internal audit, risk management, internal audit organisation and relationships with boards, audit committees and other risk functions as well as involvement in strategy.

The interviews highlight a variety of ways in which internal audit departments are structured and contribute to their companies. It shows that the Turnbull Report has done a great deal to help raise the profile of internal auditors in organisations by identifying the role that they can play in internal control and risk management, although it also shows a continuing wide variety in the role they play within their organisations. Whilst there was always variety in the way internal audit functions were organised and in the role they played, the traditional view of internal audit as a pure compliance based function, strictly enforcing the company's internal procedures and probably striking fear into the hearts of departments subject to audit visits is now untypical, but it has not been replaced by a uniform model. The variety of roles played by internal auditors and identified by this study continues to demonstrate that internal audit can provide a number of extremely useful organisational tools for management operating in a dynamic environment. I believe that the study will be of interest to many who work in Internal audit, and will be useful to many who are responsible for deciding what role it can and should best play in their organisation, whether in response to the recent changes in the Combined Code resulting from the Higgs recommendations, or simply because a fresh look is needed.

The Research Committee of the Institute of Chartered Accountants of Scotland has been happy to sponsor this project and is pleased that the research is becoming available at a time when corporate governance generally is so topical. As such, the Research Committee hopes that this project will be seen as a valuable contribution to current thinking by companies undergoing change and seeking to develop the role of their internal audit departments.

Nigel Macdonald
Convener,
Research Committee

August 2004

ACKNOWLEDGEMENT

We are indebted to many people for support and encouragement in carrying out this research project. Firstly we should like to thank the participants who gave freely of their time to be interviewed by us in the midst of their busy schedules. Many of them communicated a sense of enthusiasm for their work and its worth and intellectual challenge which is a credit to the profession of internal auditing. To preserve the confidentiality of them and their organisations we do not name them here but are nonetheless grateful to them.

The referees to the project and the ICAS Research Committee gave us valuable advice in the design of the project and in comments upon successive drafts. We are particularly grateful for the good advice and support of Professor Vivien Beattie, the Director of Research at ICAS from the beginning to almost the end of the project. Trish Watkinson at Portsmouth and Wendy Buggs at Oxford transcribed the interviews with patience and good humour. Isobel Webber became a confidante for us both as well as administering the project at ICAS and typesetting the final report.

The Research Committee and the researchers are grateful for the financial support of the Trustees of the Scottish Accountancy Research Trust without which the research would not have been possible.

Finally the researchers are grateful for the patience and support of our spouses who accepted our time devoted to the project with their usual good grace.

EXECUTIVE SUMMARY

The report of the Cadbury Committee in 1992 provided a framework for corporate governance which has become the basis for the arrangements whereby UK companies govern themselves. However, the Cadbury Report left a significant piece of unfinished business. The Code contained a recommendation that the boards of listed companies should report on the effectiveness of their systems of internal control, and that the auditors should report on this statement. This requirement was controversial, as neither company managements nor auditors were willing to take responsibility for expressing an opinion on internal control effectiveness. It was not until 1999 that the report of the Internal Control Working Party under the chairmanship of Turnbull resolved the problem of reporting on internal control.

The Turnbull Report's guidance required companies to report whether the board had reviewed the system of 'internal control and risk management', and encouraged, but did not require, the board to express an opinion on the effectiveness of the system. The close coupling of internal control and risk management in the Turnbull Report echoes similar developments in the US and Canada where other influential reports have emphasised the importance of risk management as well as internal control. Although previous research among leading companies has indicated that formal systems of risk management and risk based approaches to internal audit are in use, other research has suggested that in many companies internal audit is more traditional. In this situation there is considerable potential for a high level of adjustment costs borne by firms in complying with the Turnbull guidance, whether or not the individual firm benefits from embracing risk-based internal audit and control techniques.

At the same time the Institute of Internal Auditors has been seeking to professionalise the work of internal auditors by issuing standards of work, providing certification of education and training and enhancing the prominence of internal audit in the business community. The Cadbury Committee provided an enhancement for the role of internal audit and a presumption that listed companies would have an internal audit function, or, if not, would review the need for one periodically, the Turnbull guidance reinforced this.

Against this background, this study explores the range of activities undertaken by internal audit departments, their role within companies and the impact of the Turnbull guidance on internal audit.

The investigation uses qualitative research methods to gather the perceptions, on a wide range of issues, of senior internal auditors in large businesses, all but one being FTSE 350 companies. Between 1999 and 2001 twenty-two interviews were conducted with heads of internal audit or their deputies. The research takes a grounded theory approach and does not seek to provide statistical generalisations about the frequency of particular practices and arrangements for internal audit and risk management, but to generate understanding of the inter-relationship of different factors that are causing changes in risk management processes in companies and in the role of internal audit.

Findings from interviews with internal auditors

The interviews covered a number of issues explicitly under the following main headings:

- Turnbull and internal audit;
- Risk identification, assessment and management;
- Organisation of internal audit;
- Relationships and engagement with boards and audit committees and other risk functions;
- Involvement of internal audit in strategy.

Turnbull and internal audit

The impact of Turnbull on companies that had already embraced risk-based approaches was not perceived as very significant. The impact on some, usually smaller, companies had been greater in terms of adjustment to processes and some mention was made of increased costs. Internal auditors generally viewed Turnbull as beneficial to their cause and said it had helped to alter the perceptions of internal audit in a positive way, so that operating departments frequently sought the advice of internal audit when implementing new or changed processes.

Risk identification, assessment and management

Formalised risk management procedures were at different stages of development. The Turnbull Report had encouraged formalisation of processes in most companies, although many considered their processes 'Turnbull compliant' prior to the publication of the report. Several companies had set up risk committees. The relationship of internal audit with risk management varied from that of outside observer to influential insider. In particular, internal auditors had roles as facilitators and organisers of risk identification and assessment, generally through workshops. Risk assessment tended to be based on expected value of impact principles but the assessment was frequently summarised in the form of a score, a matrix, or 'traffic lights'. The risk identification and assessment process generally included the production of risk registers in various guises, either maintained centrally or at operating units. When adverse events occurred ('crystallisation of risk') internal audit was frequently involved in reporting on events and making recommendations for improved controls.

Organisation of internal audit

There was a wide diversity of arrangements. Some companies had dedicated internal audit functions but in most companies the function was combined with 'risk management', 'process review' or similar activities. Some auditors acknowledged a traditional compliance checking role but there was a widespread view that monitoring of compliance was a function that should, as far as possible, be the responsibility of line management.

Outsourcing of the entire internal audit function was rare in the companies examined although 'co-sourcing' arrangements, where external providers (generally audit firms) supplied expertise in specific areas such as IT, were fairly common. Outsourcing of internal audit meant forgoing most of the important educational and development benefits of internal audit and the view was generally expressed that providers of outsourced services neither understood the businesses that they were auditing nor were they committed to it in the same way as in-house staff.

The work programme of internal audit was, to a greater or lesser extent, an outcome of companies' risk identification and assessment processes in many of the companies. However, other factors, such as rotation of coverage and the priorities of the board or audit committee, also affected the design of the programme.

Relationships and engagement with boards and audit committees and other risk functions

Some boards and audit committees were more proactive than others. All the internal audit reports were made available to audit committees and all heads of internal audit attended audit committee meetings. Most companies had other risk functions apart from internal audit, such as health and safety and insurance. Where separate processes existed, the integration of risk management could only occur at the level where the lines of reporting intersected, usually at board level.

Involvement in strategy

In view of the role that external auditors seemed to be seeking as business advisers, interviewees were asked about the level of involvement of internal audit in the formation and implementation of business strategy. Internal auditors did not have, nor did they seek, a prominent role in strategic decision making, although those who were more involved with process improvement thought that they had a role in implementation.

A number of facets of internal audit emerged strongly from the interviews which were not originally included in the interview questions:

- Communication;
- Education and development;
- Independence;
- Change.

Communication

Much of the activity that internal auditors undertook could be classified as communication, especially talking with divisional and business managers, running workshops and making presentations to senior management. The workshop, in particular, seemed to be an important way in which auditors facilitated the identification and assessment of risks or dealt with other issues.

Education and development

Internal auditors saw three important educational roles: they trained their own staff, they educated line managers in control and risk management, and they provided a function where new entrants to the organisation, or existing staff, could spend a short period as a means of understanding the business. Although this feature of internal audit is well-known, the interviewees placed considerable emphasis on it.

Independence

Although a few of the interviewees fiercely guarded the independence of internal audit, refusing to accept ownership of any processes or undertake work which they felt would compromise their independence, most departments were involved in risk-management and process improvement in ways which meant that they would at some point be auditing processes that they had helped to design or implement. This qualified independence was viewed as beneficial, although auditors were conscious of the need to maintain a balance. The direct line of reporting to the audit committee was seen as reinforcing independence, and some auditors believed that they were more independent than the external auditors, whose position could be compromised by their business advisory role and their vested interest in selling additional services.

Change

During the interviews it was apparent that the work of internal audit was influenced both by frequent specific changes, such as acquisitions and divestments, and by a pervasive climate of change. In many organisations, risk-based approaches could be seen as one response to change since businesses were rarely stable long enough for processes to be designed, implemented and standardised so that a classical, systems-based approach to audit could be established. Moreover, the occurrence of specific changes provided internal audit with a role in recommending and developing processes to adapt to those changes, as well as a prioritisation, based on risk assessment, of where to expend control and risk management effort.

Implications

The diversity of the findings suggests that, although the Turnbull Report has significantly raised the profile of internal audit in organisations by highlighting its role in internal control and risk management, the organisational role of internal audit varies widely. The role as the stern enforcer of compliance with company systems has largely been abandoned, wherever it existed, but has not been replaced by a uniform model.

Internal audit provides some useful organisational tools for management in a dynamic environment:

- internal audit can identify and spread best practice, where the development of central policies would be too slow and costly;
- internal audit can gather intelligence on risks;
- internal audit can assess risks and the robustness of systems; and
- internal audit can help to maintain an organisational culture.

Risk management has become a central focus of corporate governance. Its processes provide an organisational defence in a changing environment. The interviewees told their stories against a background of continual change, including changes in organisational structure and changes in assurance requirements. In the context of new organisational paradigms, such as the concept of the learning organisation, where knowledge assets and information flows assume great significance, internal audit can potentially raise its profile greatly by emphasising its education, facilitation and communication roles.

CHAPTER ONE

INTRODUCTION

The Turnbull Report (Turnbull Committee, 1999) was the end point of a convoluted process originating from a requirement in the Cadbury Report (Cadbury Committee, 1992) for listed companies to report on their systems of internal financial control. A key feature of the Turnbull Report was the close coupling of internal control and risk management that seemed to signify a change in the way in which internal control was regarded by boards of directors and the financial reporting community.

In order to explore the impact of this change, this study is designed to investigate how the compliance and enforcement objectives of internal control are now achieved in the context of organisational risk management processes. Since internal audit is closely involved in the monitoring of internal control systems, the perceptions of internal auditors were sought on:

- the impact of the Turnbull requirements;
- the way risk is identified, assessed and managed;
- the organisation of internal audit and the extent to which internal auditors' roles have expanded and evolved to emphasise risk management;
- the relationship of internal audit with other risk management and control functions within their organisations; and
- the degree of involvement of internal audit in strategy.

Most commentators agree that internal audit has changed and is still changing in important ways. McNamee & McNamee (1995) chart the changes in internal auditing since the Second World War and describe a transformation from validation of transactions to a process of systems auditing. They also detect a change in which internal auditors have become 'a primary agent for transformational change' in helping users of systems to 'design, test and monitor their own controls'.

Such developments have certainly been recommended elsewhere. For example, in 1993, the Institute of Chartered Accountants of Scotland, in the discussion document *Auditing into the Twenty-first Century*, identified the requirement for boards of directors to report on company internal control systems as a key measure in improving the perceived effectiveness of financial audit. The report recommended a greatly strengthened role for internal audit teams, whose work would complement that of external audit, offering a more integrated provision of assurance to boards to underpin directors' reporting on internal controls.

It is not yet known to what extent such changes have in fact become pervasive within organisations. There is some evidence that organisations known for their leading edge risk-management practices (Selim & McNamee, 1999) have an alignment of risk-management and internal audit practice but the authors acknowledge that this is by no means universal and they suggest that a range of changes in the culture and competencies of internal audit functions will need to be made if they are to go in the same direction. The Selim and McNamee model of risk-management starts with risk-assessment and is followed by risk-management and risk communication; in this model internal audit is derived *from* the strategic planning process rather than being a process that contributes *to* strategy formation. Blackburn (1999), an experienced practitioner, develops a similar normative model in a publication designed to assist auditors to implement Turnbull; risk assessment is conducted through an analysis of the value chain for business processes. Blackburn recommends a 'five forces' model and a PEST environmental analysis (which explores political, economic, sociocultural and technological influences) as techniques for the assessment of strategic risk. Other approaches to risk identification and management have been proposed such as the Arthur Andersen model (ICAEW Steering Group on the Financial Reporting of Risk, 1999) which seeks to identify risks from an inventory of types of risks rather than by focusing on business processes.

Surveying finance directors of large listed companies, Griffiths (1999) found that they viewed internal audit as 'too low key and basic (and therefore insufficiently business risk-oriented)' and lacking in skills or appropriately trained staff.

Recognising a range of internal audit orientations to risk, Deloitte and Touche Tohmatsu (2000) asserted:

> *The shift in the risk-control landscape creates both challenges and opportunities for internal auditors. Those that handle the challenge quickly and cost-effectively will be credited with helping their organisation meet its business goals. Those that don't will be left behind, stranded in a world where the attitude 'you are either part of the problem or part of the solution' separates the survivors from the casualties. There is still much work to be done and we hope that internal audit professionals will see beyond today and carve a vision worthy of tomorrow.* (p.6)

There is thus some evidence that, although advocates of internal audit claim a position at the heart of risk management, in practice many internal audit departments may not have embraced risk-based approaches. Nor is it proven that risk-based approaches are always appropriate. It is possible that Turnbull compliance may involve significant adjustment costs for companies.

Risk management

The conception of risk as manageable is a modern phenomenon, only made possible by the development of scientific techniques that enable the calculation of the likelihood and impact of events. In pre-modern society, adverse events that we would now associate with risk were more likely to be viewed as the workings of 'Fate' or 'Acts of God', beyond the influence of human intervention.

As risk became more manageable through measurement and quantification, strategies of avoidance and protection (through financial compensation, for example) became possible. Beck's (1998) conception of the 'risk society' presents a world in which accountability, as well as risk, is manageable. He argues that the processes of risk management mask responsibility, making accountability diffuse and difficult to determine. In contrast to this view, the corporate governance debate presents risk-management as a mechanism for making accountability more transparent.

A significant element in risk-management is awareness by organisational participants of the likely personal consequences of a risk crystallising in the form of an adverse event. Douglas (1986; 1992) has analysed the role of the attribution of misfortune in society, demonstrating that blame is central to social and organisational structures. In pre-modern society, blame was closely associated with systems of justice and had a distinct moral connection, but Douglas argues that the development of sophisticated risk analysis has broken this link, although blame still retains a vital organisational role:

> The central method of monitoring is to fasten attention on misfortunes … Any major mishap in an organisation sparks off questions about responsibility. Processes of blame-pinning or exonerating from blame strengthen the pattern of the organisation and are actually an integral part of it. (Douglas, 1986, pp.84-85)

Avoidance of blame and liability remains a powerful influence in the design of risk-regulation regimes (Hood *et al*, 2001, p.176).

Even though the possibility of risk management is now generally accepted, conceptualisations of risk range along a continuum from objective (technico-scientific) to social constructionist views, a range clearly illustrated in the disagreement between physical and social scientists involved in preparing the Royal Society's 1992 report *Risk: Analysis, Perception and Management* (Adams, 1995, p.7; Douglas, 1999, p.218). Hood *et al*. (2001) analyse risk regulation regimes and demonstrate that varying notions of risk will lead to different assumptions about the ways in which it may be regulated and managed. This has particular significance within organisations, where disparate risks may be subject to different management processes in different parts of the organisation. By defining risk and its management to suit their own ends, interest groups may seek to increase their power.

Corporate governance rhetoric presents risk as objectively identifiable, quantifiable and strategically manageable. (The recent US exposure draft *Enterprise Risk Management Framework* (COSO, 2004), is an example.) A lack of recognition of the disparity in approaches to the conception of risk could have a significant impact on both the success of mechanisms designed to improve accountability, such as the Turnbull guidance, and on the position of organisational actors, such as internal auditors. This possibility formed one impetus for this investigation.

The Sarbanes-Oxley Act

At the time that the research was undertaken the significance of the Enron and WorldCom affairs was only beginning to emerge. One outcome of the scandals has been the enactment in the US of the Sarbanes-Oxley Act which contains a number of sweeping provisions. In particular, the management of listed companies in the US will be required to present an opinion on the effectiveness of their systems of internal control. As noted in chapter two, the speed of enactment and scope of these provisions contrast markedly with the protracted debate which has resulted in the less stringent provisions on reporting on internal control in the UK.

The monograph structure

This chapter has described the background to the study with reference to prior research on the role of internal audit and to the development of the concept of risk-management. Chapter two provides more detail about the context of the study, outlining how the Turnbull guidance arose from the development of corporate governance policy within the UK and discussing how risk-management has become associated with internal control and the development of internal audit functions within businesses. The chapter ends by identifying the research questions which form the basis of the inquiry.

Chapter three explains the research approach, the analysis of the preliminary interviews with internal auditors and the development of the research instrument.

Chapter four presents a model of the relationship between the approaches to risk management of companies and of their internal auditors, identifying influences on the extent of involvement of internal audit in risk management.

Chapter five presents an analysis of the interview data, exploring, within our interviewees' organisations, the impact of the Turnbull requirements, the way risk is identified, assessed and managed, the organisation of internal audit, the relationship of internal audit with other risk management and control functions and the degree of involvement of internal audit in strategy.

Chapter six develops further themes – education, communication, independence and change - which emerged during the analysis of interviews and which provide different insights into the role of internal audit and risk management.

Chapter seven sets out the conclusions of the investigation.

CHAPTER TWO

THE CONTEXT OF THE STUDY

This chapter describes the origins and development of the Turnbull guidance and outlines existing evidence about the role of internal audit in risk-management which provides a basis for the formulation of the research questions underpinning this study.

The origins and development of the Turnbull guidance

Corporate governance policy in the UK has focused on improvements in internal control, based on the assumption that a relationship exists between internal control, financial reporting quality and corporate governance standards, although commentators such as Maijoor (2000) have noted that this assumption remains untested.

Internal control practice changed markedly in the latter part of the twentieth century, influenced by the introduction of new technology and changes in audit approach. Auditors argue that information technology systems are now so reliable that detailed checking of transaction recording is unnecessary, although the systems themselves, including the inherent controls, may be poorly documented and barely understood, this is reflected in the fact that IT auditors are highly sought after in internal audit departments. The shift in external audit focus to a business risk approach has also led to a significant reduction in systems documentation and testing (Lemon *et al*, 2000). The adoption of new management concepts such as "the learning organisation" and techniques such as business process re-engineering have combined with these influences to change internal control practice: top-down control structures have been replaced by devolved systems in which control is subordinated to systems of risk management. Concomitantly, demands for improved transparency in financial reporting have shifted the corporate governance focus from the financial control remit of the Cadbury Committee to embrace a requirement for wider disclosure of all business risks (ICAEW, 1997; ICAEW Steering Group on the Financial Reporting of Risk, 1999).

> *The developing importance of internal control within the worldwide corporate governance debate can be traced back to the US Treadway Report of 1987 which addressed the problem of fraudulent financial reporting from a perspective of internal control, and was followed in 1992 by the COSO report, produced by the Committee of Sponsoring Organisations of the Treadway Report, which set out a framework for the establishment and evaluation of organisational internal control systems. The COSO definition of internal control extends beyond the financial remit, as does the more recent Criteria on Control (CoCo) framework produced by the Canadian Institute of Chartered Accountants in 1995. Problems of interpretation of the meaning of internal control remain: Maijoor (2000) explores the implications of the lack of clear definitions and boundaries in the European context, suggesting that this lack of clarity leads to corporate governance policy decisions based on untested assumptions. For example, there is as yet no evidence that reporting on internal control improves corporate governance standards.* (Hermanson, 2000)

The history of the development of the Combined Code illustrates the increasing importance of internal control in the UK. The Cadbury Report recommended that 'directors should make a statement in the report and accounts on the effectiveness of their system of internal control and that the auditors should report thereon' (Cadbury Committee, 1992, 4.32). Cadbury charged the accountancy profession with the task of developing criteria for assessing effectiveness and practical guidance for directors as to how to formulate and present such reports. However, the vagueness of the concept of internal control effectiveness made directors understandably reluctant to report (Power, 1997, p.55).

The first attempt to provide guidance was the 1994 Rutteman Report, which defined internal financial control as 'the internal controls established in order to provide reasonable assurance of: (a) the safeguarding of assets against unauthorised use or disposition; and (b) the maintenance of proper accounting records and the reliability of financial information used within the business or for publication' (Rutteman Committee, 1994).

The Cadbury prescription that directors **should** report on internal control effectiveness was replaced in section eight of Rutteman by the suggestion that they **may wish** to do so. Chambers (1997) suggests that lobbying by finance directors who feared litigation led to this weakening of the Cadbury recommendations. The Hampel Committee (1998) revisited the issues covered by Cadbury and took a different perspective:

> *The importance of corporate governance lies in its contribution both to business prosperity and to accountability. In the UK the latter has preoccupied much public debate over the past few years. We would wish to see the balance corrected. ... the emphasis on accountability has tended to obscure a board's first responsibility – to enhance the prosperity of the business over time.* (Hampel Committee, 1998, p.7)

The tone of the report conveys the clear belief that governance and accountability measures do not enhance entrepreneurial activity, although no evidence is provided to support this view (Bruce, 1998).

The Combined Code, which followed Hampel, included explicit statements about the role of the board in relation to internal control:

The board should maintain a sound system of internal control to safeguard shareholders' investment and the company's assets. (Principle D.2)

The directors should, at least annually, conduct a review of the effectiveness of the group's system of internal control and should report to shareholders that they have done so. The review should cover all controls, including financial, operational and compliance controls and risk management. (Provision D.2.1)

The guidance for directors envisaged by Cadbury was finally provided by the Turnbull Committee (Turnbull Committee, 1999). Turnbull identified the elements of a 'sound' system of internal control and outlined a process whereby boards could fulfil their responsibilities to report on this area.

There is some linking of risk management and internal control in Hampel, which was not present in the Cadbury report, but Turnbull makes the association explicit. This approach is reinforced by advice to directors on Turnbull compliance (Jones & Sutherland, 1999). These developments are summarised in the following table:

Table 2.1 Scope and requirement for reporting on internal control
effectiveness in UK corporate governance guidance

	Cadbury	Rutteman	Hampel	Turnbull
Scope	Internal financial control	Internal financial control	Internal control (all controls, including financial, operational and compliance controls and risk management)	Internal control and risk management
Reporting	Effectiveness	Review undertaken may report on effectiveness	Review undertaken	Review undertaken

Source: Spira & Page, 2003

The trend away from a narrow internal control scope with a high level of reporting requirements towards a broader scope with less stringent reporting is illustrated thus:

Table 2.2 Trend in scope and reporting requirements

```
┌─────────────────────────────────────────────────────────────────┐
│  SCOPE                                                            │
│                                                                   │
│   Broad     ▲                                                     │
│             │COSO                                                 │
│             │CoCo      TURNBULL                                   │
│             │          HAMPEL                                     │
│             │                    ──────────────────────          │
│             │                    RUTTEMAN                         │
│             │                         CADBURY                     │
│   Narrow    │                                                     │
│             │                                    REPORTING        │
│             └──────────────────────────────────▶ REQUIREMENTS     │
│              Low                       High                       │
│                                                                   │
└─────────────────────────────────────────────────────────────────┘
```

Source: Spira & Page, 2003

The long and stately debate which centred on whether UK directors should report on the soundness of the system of internal control has been not been mirrored in the US where, in the wake of the Enron debacle and other *causes celebres*, the Sarbanes–Oxley Act has required a report of 'management's assessment, as of the end of the company's most recent fiscal year, of the effectiveness of the company's internal control structure and procedures for financial reporting (section 404)'[1] together with a report of the auditors on the management's assessment. Although the Act refers to 'disclosure controls', in practice management will need to attest to the effectiveness of the whole system of internal control and risk management and the management report will need to be audited annually, if current proposals by the SEC come into force. These stringent requirements would put the US position in the top right hand corner of the diagram, in contrast with the UK position that only has a narrow focus. Many UK companies which are required to make SEC filings will therefore need to comply (PricewaterhouseCoopers, 2003).

There remains some confusion about the relationship between internal control and risk management. Is control a part of risk management or is risk management an element of control? According to the Canadian Institute of Chartered Accountants Criteria of Control Board 'Control should cover the identification and mitigation of risks' (Canadian Institute of Chartered Accountants, 1999, p.9). Similarly, the COSO framework identified risk assessment as one of the five components of internal control. Turnbull, however, stated that 'A company's system of internal control has a key role in the management of risks that are significant to the fulfilment of its business objectives' (Turnbull Committee, 1999, p.4). Blackburn (1999, p.36) argues that the artificial separation of risk management and internal control from business operations is the source of this confusion.

The shift to a focus on risk management avoids the difficulty of defining internal control and links neatly to the re-focusing of the corporate governance debate from improving financial reporting quality to a concern that corporate governance mechanisms should not impede enterprise (Short *et al*, 1999). The Hampel report argued that the positive view of risk which underpins enterprise was being hampered by the regulation of the downside of risk through internal control. The conceptualisation of internal control as a risk management process characterises it as a support for enterprise through links to strategy formulation, simultaneously glossing over the uncomfortable vagueness of the definition of internal control. Turnbull has thus extended the requirements for directors to report on the broad range of risks experienced by companies, rather than the more limited range of internal financial control. However, business, operational or compliance risks may have previously been seen as the province of different departments within companies (Lilley & Saleh, 1999). In order to comply with Turnbull in a cost-effective way, companies may seek to combine dispersed areas of risk assessment and risk management, possibly resulting in competition among those involved for the position of leading advisor within the arena of this "internal regulatory space" (Power, 1999a, p.17). Internal audit is well-placed to take the advantage here: 'Other assurance functions are not usually positioned in the organisation and reporting structure with the same overview and degree of independence as internal audit', (ICAEW, 2000, p.9). Some internal audit functions have already expanded to include specialists such as engineers and marketers, providing a broader operational perspective on risk.

Internal audit and risk management

The Turnbull Report appears to have provided a significant opportunity for internal audit to demonstrate its potential to add value, to break away from its historical characterisation as the 'organisational policeman and watchdog' (Morgan, 1979, p.161), to defend its position in the face of challenges such as outsourcing and to define itself as a distinctive profession.

Internal auditors have sought recognition of their professional status over a long period of time (Kalbers & Fogarty, 1995). As long ago as 1979, Morgan observed that:

> ... recent IIA pronouncements which emphasise how internal audit should provide a "service to the organisation" and how internal auditors should become more accountable to Audit Committees of Boards of Directors and society, rather than exclusively to management ... signal the definition of a role and power base which returns to the philosophy of the original audit role ... but which carries with it an expanded conception of the audit function which ... seeks to combine control and advisory functions, by orienting the latter to the highest organisational levels. (Morgan, 1979, pp.169-70)

Twenty years after Morgan's observations, a new definition of internal auditing from the Institute of Internal Auditors identified an assurance and consulting role for internal audit and emphasised adding value and improving the effectiveness of risk management, control and governance processes through qualities of independence and objectivity. While this potential contribution to corporate objectives offers an opportunity for a stronger claim to professional status by internal audit, the tension remains between the consultancy role and the claims of independence on which this status relies. Competition from other specialists in audit and risk management may still be fierce. As Pentland (2000) observed, auditors are experts in process rather than content: in areas such as environmental audit, specialists from other disciplines may challenge the expert status of the traditional internal auditor.

Fogarty and Kalbers (2000, p.134) identified independence, autonomy and self-regulation as key attributes in the professionalisation process, but observed that '… organisations should also be aware that internal auditing inherently involves role conflict. Efforts to eliminate role conflict may deny internal auditors the very essence of their roles in the organisations'.

The financial scandals which provoked world-wide concern with corporate governance in the 1990s, and the more recent examples such as Enron, highlighted apparent failures of accountability mechanisms, including audit and internal control, which have become a focus for the debate about reform. Directors seeking assurance about corporate governance practice are likely to develop a new regard for the expertise of internal auditors in the crucial area of risk management. How far have internal auditors taken advantage of this opportunity?

As noted in chapter one, there is certainly evidence demonstrating that they aspire to this reframing of their role in terms of risk management: examples are offered by the new definition of internal auditing issued by the Institute of Internal Auditors in June 1999[2], as well as commentary in recent articles (*eg* (Bou-Raad, 2000; Chambers,

2000)). References to risk in professional journals and in newsletters relating to internal audit over the last five years have been observed, as well as an increasing focus on risk in the titles of articles therein (Chambers, 2000).

However, the extent to which this aspiration is being achieved remains unclear. Surveys by KPMG in the US (KPMG, 1999) and Deloitte and Touche Tohmatsu in New Zealand (Deloitte and Touche Tohmatsu, 2000) suggest that internal auditors are more optimistic about the extent of their potential contribution to risk assessment and management than are senior executives. UK studies raise similar doubts (Griffiths, 1999; Selim & McNamee, 1999).

Summary

This review of the developing role of internal audit in relation to risk management led to the formulation of the following broad research questions:

- Has the Turnbull Report requirement for directors to report on internal control and risk management necessitated any organisational changes and to what extent have internal auditors been involved?

- How do companies approach risk identification, assessment and management?

- How is internal audit organised?

- How does internal audit contribute to business risk management and relate to other risk functions within organisations?

- What input do internal auditors perceive that they have to strategic management decision making?

In this chapter the origins of the Turnbull guidance in the UK corporate governance debate have been outlined and its potential impact on the development of internal audit has been discussed, providing a context for the formulation of the research questions that this study seeks to illuminate. The following chapter describes the research method adopted to explore these questions.

ENDNOTES:

---

[1] See http://www.sec.gov/news/press/2003-66.htm.

[2] 'Internal auditing is an independent, objective assurance and consulting activity designed to add value and improve an organisation's operations. It helps an organisation accomplish its objectives by bringing a systematic, disciplined approach to evaluate and improve the effectiveness of risk management, control and governance processes.' (see http://www.iia.org.uk/about/internalaudit/)

CHAPTER THREE

RESEARCH METHOD

In this chapter the research method used to undertake the study is described and the data derived from two preliminary interviews is discussed and the subsequent two-phase interview process is also noted.

Grounded theory

The relative lack of previous research into internal audit and risk management indicated that a qualitative research approach was an appropriate way to investigate the impact of the Turnbull Report and current developments in internal audit. A grounded theory approach was adopted because its increasing acceptance within the accounting literature meant that it would be readily interpretable (Parker & Roffey, 1997). Grounded theory aims to arrive at theories about events and social processes from a position of minimum prior assumptions and theory. It can be applied to a wide range of different kinds of data including archive material, participant observation and interviews. In view of the need to cover a spectrum of organisations in the work, it was decided to conduct semi-structured interviews.

Like all qualitative research methods, grounded theory has been criticised for its relative lack of objectivity and replicability. Since grounded theory requires intensive analysis of relatively few sources (in this case, interviews) its results are not generalisable in a statistical sense: it is not possible to say with confidence that the characteristics of the sample will be reproduced in the whole population. Rather, grounded theory aims for 'theoretical generalisation' in the sense that the outcome is a richer theory of events and processes which can be taken further in other work.

Although some grounded theorists claim to conduct research on the basis of a completely blank sheet so far as prior theorising is concerned, this is, in the view of the authors, not completely practical. Merely by choosing to research a particular topic, the researcher is implicitly assuming that events have some significance and it is impossible to shed prior knowledge and training. In order to form a basis for conducting a series of interviews preliminary interviews with senior internal auditors were conducted in dissimilar organisations.

The preliminary interviews

Pilot interviews with two senior internal auditors were conducted who illustrated contrasting approaches to internal audit. A detailed account is provided here to demonstrate the way in which the model is grounded in the data collected.

One internal auditor came from a diversified UK group with manufacturing, retailing and service automotive segments (Company U). The other came from an international manufacturing group within the agricultural, paper and packaging industrial classification (Company T). Company U faced a range of commercial and health and safety risks common to a wide spectrum of companies but company T faced a number of political, social and environmental risks in its markets which were high profile and difficult to manage[1]. The company U internal auditor is characterised as taking a risk management based approach, while the internal auditor at company T operated in a more traditional way.

The risk-based auditor (RIA)

The risk-based auditor, RIA, took an almost evangelical stance to risk-management. RIA had a strong commitment to change. In part of the group, internal auditing had been outsourced to a Big Five firm but in RIA's view this had not worked because the staff employed on the actual audit were too junior to 'engage' with the management of the business, so that although the audit provided assurance, it did not lead to change.

RIA's operating style was very people oriented. RIA viewed the operations of the company as the outcome of personal interactions between various actors within it and outside it. To this end, internal auditors needed to be a team and to be viewed as such by the rest of the company, despite geographical dispersion and a range of expertise (not every member of the team was a qualified accountant). RIA discussed the importance of 'incidents' (risks that happen) in defining attitudes to risk. It was important to avoid a blame culture; incidents should be used as a basis for learning rather than apportioning blame.

RIA viewed internal audit as distinct from the finance function but had been unsuccessful in the wish to report to the managing director rather than the financial director.

RIA summed up the approach to internal audit in Company U: 'we do not do fieldwork to find out what is going on, to provide assurance. I believe we do fieldwork so that we raise the level of the knowledge of the generalist internal auditor sufficient to engage in facilitated dialogue with management'.

The basis of risk assessment in company U was Porter's value chain: the processes of the business were divided into different functional areas and the risks associated with them assessed. RIA viewed risk as difficult to quantify and capture. It was not possible to rely solely on the managers of different subsidiaries to describe the risks; there was a need to 'dig down' to capture 'lower levels' of risk. The internal audit team had some difficulty in persuading managers of this. Subsidiary managers seemed to want internal audit to work on their systems and were sometimes reluctant to spend time with internal auditors on the discussion and identification of risk. RIA was endeavouring to introduce a change in the company's expectations of internal audit:"It has also been a question of getting the management of the subsidiaries and the centre used to the idea of 'Now we are not going out to write a finance controls manual for you, no, we are not going to tick against your financial controls manual'".

The role of internal auditor was intended as non-threatening to subsidiaries: it was more 'comfortable ... , challenging but comfortable' (although it is not known whether auditees saw it in the same light).

RIA did not seem to have to compete with other functions in the company for the 'turf' of risk assessment. Possible 'competing' disciplines, such as the company secretariat and the 'risk manager' dealing with insurance, seemed to have been happy to adopt the framework provided by internal audit. Health and safety risks were important to Company U but they had been shunted into various functional areas rather than competed for. On RIA's part there was no great eagerness for empire building - for example, RIA thought the risk manager should report through the treasury function rather than through internal audit. Risk had not been dominated by finance thinking: the company did not seem to incorporate risk into its capital expenditure approval process and RIA thought that it should. The control policy for the treasury function seemed to be 'old-fashioned' and not to have caught up with the great range of financial instruments now available. There had been an 'incident' which had brought this to light.

The Turnbull Report had helped RIA to implement the risk-based approach since it was necessary for management to undertake risk assessments. The previous approach had been based on internal controls rather than internal controls growing out of risk assessments.

RIA was surprised at the attitude of the audit committee to risk. The culture was one of requiring answers rather than of questioning. The committee did not want to be bothered with 'all this "boring corporate governance stuff"'. The chairman of the committee seemed reluctant to spend time with RIA.

RIA saw ethical issues as integral with the risk approach. The service element of the business critically depended on being seen to be ethical and in possession of integrity. This view may have been at odds with the thinking of many of the managers of local depots. Many of these managers had been in much smaller, budget constrained organisations only a very few years previously, before they were taken over by company U. RIA admitted that the organisation had a very strong budget culture which instilled 'a culture of fear and scarcity' into some managers so that they were reluctant to invest even in necessary health and safety improvements. Despite the reluctance of subsidiaries to invest in health and safety, these issues were handled differently from other risks since they were reported direct to the board rather than through the audit committee. RIA felt health and safety could not be isolated from other risks, however; an integrated approach to risk was necessary and risk management needed to be 'embedded' within the management process.

The traditional auditor (TIA)

The group internal auditor from Company T, TIA, worked in a regime where risk management was a management process, not an internal audit process. The company had audit committees at subsidiary, regional and main board levels which followed organisational structure closely. Risk management was delegated to subsidiary management who were tasked with identifying and addressing risks, including formulating action plans in case 'events' or 'occurrences' happened. The group had a system of 'risk registers' which were reviewed by audit committees. The role of internal audit was to second guess the management's assessment of business risk (in the sense of failure to achieve objectives) and audit test the risks and the effectiveness of critical controls. Risk was dealt with in terms of risk to objectives rather than being classified functionally or by type of risk. Internal auditors did not do financial auditing; TIA saw their role as conducting business risk audits. Thus, while TIA did not conduct audits that were traditional in the sense of involving substantive testing, TIA's position in relation to auditees was far more like that of the traditional conception of the internal auditor than that of RIA.

There had been a significant change in the work of the internal auditor in company T in the last five years which had coincided with the setting up of the audit committee structure. Previously the work had been more compliance based but now the focus was business risk.

Internal auditors were high fliers who generally spent two to three years in internal audit in order to get a whole business view before returning to line management. They were drawn from a range of disciplines, whereas before the restructuring they were mainly accountants. Subsidiaries appreciated the development potential of internal audit for their people and were willing to assign high fliers to internal audit for a period.

Audit committees were important in the risk management process since there was a risk presentation to each audit committee at least once a year identifying key risks. TIA emphasised the importance of communication and audit committee meetings were an important mechanism for communicating information about risk throughout the group. Audit committees dealt with a rolling programme of key issues.

Internal audit could be stressful for the companies undergoing a review. New financial directors or general managers frequently welcomed internal audit to give them an overview of problems, but after a couple of years in the job they viewed the prospect of internal audit with some concern. Subsidiaries often had their own internal audit departments and one of the tasks of group internal audit was to evaluate the self-sufficiency of subsidiaries' internal audit departments: if they were not good enough, group internal audit would undertake some of the tasks with them. More than once TIA characterised the outcome of internal audit as 'getting the issues out on the table' so that management could address them. TIA stressed that audit committees were interactive and that they asked questions rather than seeking to have identification of issues neatly packaged with solutions.

Ethical issues were quite important to Company T. The group had an ethics policy and tried to comply with the law and corporate governance requirements in each of its countries of operation. The legal department took responsibility for compliance with law, regulations and the ethical code. Changes in regulations governing the products was a considerable risk factor but contingency plans were formed, reviewed and updated.

The main board of the company was not involved in the management of routine risks but there was considerable overlap with the audit committee so that board members were kept informed. There was no demand for a separate risk committee – the chief internal auditor had 'Risk Management' as part of the job title and the function was covered by the audit committees. In some regions the internal auditor team included a person with the function 'risk manager' whose job was to organise 'bottom up' risk assessments carried out by relatively junior risk identification teams who would then be followed up by more senior 'risk evaluation' teams. Risk managers were also responsible for transferring risk through insurance.

Treasury risks were handled separately by a treasury committee. There were voluminous regulations and authority levels. The risk of a rogue trader was avoided by separation of duties – the same person could not initiate and execute a transaction.

TIA thought that the group's systems were 'Turnbull compliant' and had been since restructuring of the audit committees; they had had the systems reviewed by various governance experts and were quite confident. The prospect of additional disclosures about risk in the annual report was not a matter of great concern, in TIA's opinion, except where information might be of use to competitors.

RIA and TIA compared and contrasted

While both the senior internal auditors spoke a language of risk, it was apparent that the roles of their respective departments were different.

In company U, internal audit sought to be central to the risk management process, which was itself becoming central to the methodology of management. Internal audit was moving into a vacuum which, for a group assembled from companies with diverse businesses and procedures, needed to be filled in order to integrate its constituent parts. In this group, the vision of internal audit as strategic advisers to the board had some potential for fulfilment.

In contrast, Company T, a group with a long history and a limited range of product groups but with worldwide operations, had retained risk management in the line of managerial control. Internal audit performed a staff function but, like the external auditors, was viewing the action at a distance; it observed the players of the game rather than being one of them, despite the presence of capable people.

The causes of this difference may lie both in the nature of the companies' businesses and their states of organisational development. Company T is a business where risks are large but well-understood. It is unlikely that risk assessments will provide any surprises but risk is too important to be left to internal auditors: it is the essence of the management of the enterprise. Company T is also highly evolved;

its structure is robust and there is no managerial vacuum for internal audit to colonise.

Company U faces risks that are moderate, but poorly identified and assessed. As an accumulation of some smaller businesses which had unstructured managements, it needs to catch up with regulations and modern standards while at the same time adopting common systems and policies. In this situation, the vacuum of risk assessment and the context of ongoing organisational change offer internal audit an opportunity for colonisation.

The preliminary interviews provided a valuable insight into the workings of internal audit and risk management and sensitised the authors to the following issues, which broadened the focus of the original research questions in some respects to include:

- The role of internal audit in identifying and assessing risk.

- Different formalisations of risk management processes.

- Different levels of integration of risk based approaches in:

  - internal audit;
  - organisational management approach; and
  - the possibility of different relationships between internal audit and the organisation as a consequence.

- The role of internal audit in strategy formation and implementation.

A prior reading of the Turnbull Report and the relevant literature together with the study of the preliminary interviews, formed the tentative view that there was likely to be considerable diversity among the approaches to, and the development of, internal audit, even among leading companies. The requirement to implement Turnbull would accordingly have a differing impact upon each company. It was conjectured that the role of internal audit would be conditioned by a company's overall approach to risk, its corporate governance arrangements such as the audit committee remit, and the culture and skills of the internal audit department.

The differences between these two accounts of internal audit work suggested that it would be helpful to plot the continuum of internal audit approaches against the company approaches to risk management in a way that might frame the range of relationships between internal audit and risk management. This model was tested in subsequent interviews and is discussed in detail in chapter four.

On the basis of this theoretical sensitisation a list of topics was developed to form the basis of further semi-structured interviews with a sample of heads of internal audit across a range of industry sectors.

First phase of interviews

Ten interviews were conducted in the first phase of interviewing. These interviews were conducted with internal auditors who had largely been identified as personal contacts of the researchers or because of their participation in events such as internal audit conferences. The interviewees were mainly in large organisations with well-developed internal audit functions.

Interviews were arranged by telephone after sending an initial contact letter which specified the interest in internal audit, risk management and the Turnbull Report. After the interview had been arranged the interviewees were sent a request for further information and background material which indicated the scope of topics for discussion (Appendix One). All interviewees were guaranteed anonymity for themselves and their organisations. Several of them expressed the view that their organisations would not have allowed them to take part in the research if this were not the case.

After the first phase of interviews, some preliminary analysis of the data was undertaken that was written up as a conference presentation. The importance of various forms of communication, particularly workshops, and of education and development in the work of internal auditors, was identified at this stage.

Second phase of interviews

A second phase of interviewing was undertaken with a further ten companies. These companies were selected from the middle of the FTSE 250 index on a judgemental basis that excluded financial companies but which otherwise aimed for a spread of companies across manufacturing and service sectors. As the internal audit arrangements and key personnel were not known these companies were initially contacted by telephone to find out the name of the head of internal audit and then by a personally addressed letter which was in turn followed up by a telephone call. About half of the companies contacted were willing to take part in the research. In other cases companies refused mainly on the grounds that there was a company policy of not taking part in research projects. Once companies agreed to take part, the procedure was the same as for the first phase of interviews.

Analysis of the interviews

The interviews were transcribed from tape recordings or, in four cases, detailed notes. The first stage of the analysis was to summarise the individual interviews. This was done by using the outline facility on a word processor and summarising the interview into headings defined by the progress of the interview. Often this followed the pattern of the research instrument but sometimes it did not, where interviewees developed a line of thinking or introduced novel views. The summaries served to ground each researcher fully in the data, including the interviews conducted by the other researcher. The second stage of the analysis was to code the interviews into 'grids'. Each grid was constructed as a table within an HTML document with three columns for 'concepts', 'categories' and 'properties and dimensions'. The purpose of constructing the grids in HTML was to facilitate navigation about the document and the insertion of links between concepts. The initial grids were voluminous since the left hand column contained many concepts. The building of the initial grids was based on the original interview transcripts using the summaries only to identify initial category descriptors for each grid.

The final stage of the analysis was to construct summaries of the grids which are reproduced at appendix two. In these grids the concepts have been further refined ('selective coding' in grounded theory terms) and categories assigned to groups of concepts together with identification of associated dimensions and properties.

The grids form the basis of the analysis and description of the interviews which follows in the next two chapters. Chapter four also discusses the testing of the model of the relationships between internal audit and company approaches to risk management and sets out an analysis of the matters covered under the headings appearing in the research instrument.

ENDNOTE:

---

[1] The interviews were conducted in January 2000. T is a FTSE 100 company. U is a FTSE 250 company

CHAPTER FOUR

INTERNAL AUDITORS AND RISK MANAGEMENT PROCESSES

In this chapter a model is developed of the relationship between company and internal audit approaches to risk management. Further insights into the forces driving the dynamic identified in this model are then provided by the detailed analysis of the interviews which follows.

Approaches to risk management

Smallman (1996) describes the interconnecting influences on risk management of organisational structure, strategy and culture. He contrasts the reactionary or homeostatic approach in which risk management is limited to acceptance of consequential loss or transfer (*eg* through insurance) with the proactive or holistic approach in which risk management strategies are focused on avoidance, prevention and mitigation. The latter is characteristic of a company culture which is consultative and involving, recognising qualitative factors and viewing system failures as a learning mechanism used to influence organisational design. In the reactionary environment, risk is the province of experts alone, understood principally through quantification, and the response to system failure is attribution of blame: organisational design is not responsive to accumulated knowledge.

As previously noted an analysis of the two preliminary interviews suggested that it would be helpful to plot internal audit approaches, defined as traditional or risk-oriented, against company approaches to risk management.

Following Smallman (1996), the words reactive and holistic are used to contrast the extremes in this scale which run between the contrasting approaches of TIA and RIA drawn from the data. Plotted in matrix form, a model is derived of internal audit categories:

Figure 4.1

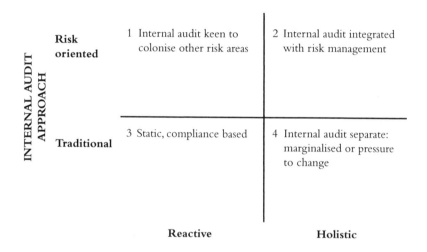

In this matrix, company U would fall into box 1, with RIA's aspiration to move the board's view of internal audit to the more integrated situation of box 2. Company T would be sited in box 4.

In order to test the model outlined on the previous page, interviewees were asked to identify their company's present position on the following scales:

Figure 4.2

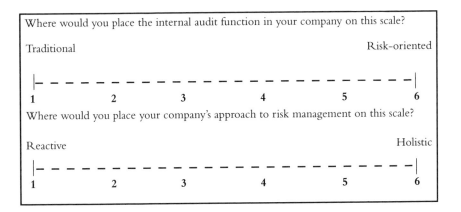

Interviewees were than asked if the resultant plotting of their response within the matrix was an accurate reflection in terms of the situation posited. The 2x2 model provided a useful heuristic for interviewees to reflect on broader issues surrounding risk management and the internal audit role. Figure 4.3 shows the self-placement of interviewees within the matrix[1].

Figure 4.3

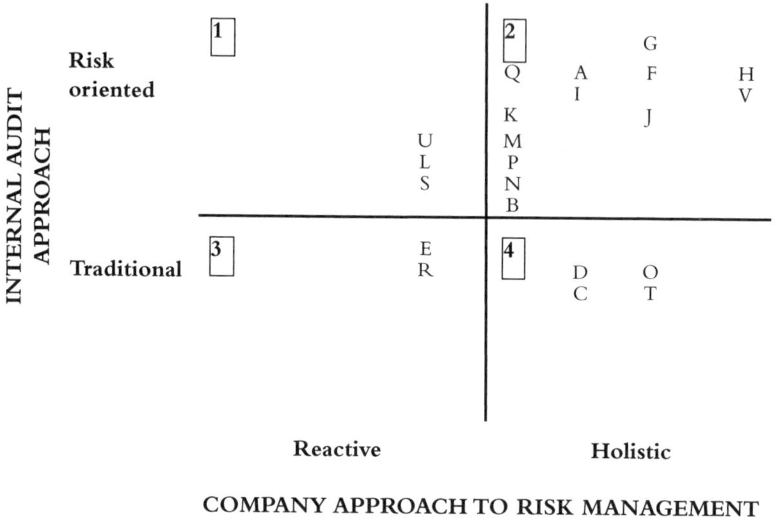

KEY:

1   Internal audit keen to colonise other risk areas
2   Internal audit integrated with risk management
3   Static, compliance based
4   Internal audit separate: marginalised or pressure to change

Companies (p = preliminary, 1 = first tranche of interviews, 2 = second)

A1	beverages	L2	support services
B1	chemicals	M1	telecommunications
C1	food	N2	media and photography
D2	engineering	O2	aerospace and defence
E2	publishing	P2	retail
F1	utility 1	Q1	transport
G1	utility 2	R1	health
H1	leisure industry	S1	construction
I2	retail	Tp	agriculture, paper and packaging
J2	distributors	Up	automotive
K2	transport	V2	telecommunications

The interviewees confirmed that box 2 – internal audit fully integrated with risk management – was the position to which internal audit would aspire and this was where most placed themselves.

Because internal auditors are professional individuals and have a judgemental scope they are bound to be risk oriented – everybody wants to be. (R)

The top right-hand corner position was described as one in which risk management was "in the bloodstream" or "baked into the walls". Most of those towards the left of box 2 described an ongoing process of integration which they believed would eventually move them further towards the top right-hand corner, although one suggested that it was probably unachievable in totality other than in a financial services context where risk management was very formalised and central to operations.

The extent of integration varied in accordance with organisational structure and the level of centralisation:

The extent to which internal audit would ever be what I would call fully integrated within risk management within the group, I think is probably debatable. The nature of the group is that we have an awful lot of delegated responsibility and business unit management have full responsibility for managing risks within their businesses. Divisional management has full responsibility for managing risks within their divisions. It is their responsibility and because of that, I think, one of the impacts of that is that there is no really strong group way of doing things. (J)

For many, the concept of internal audit integration with risk management centred around the generation of the internal audit programme from the risk management process and their own direct involvement with the risk management process, through control self assessment workshops and other facilitative and educational activities.

Few reflected on the implications of this integration for internal audit independence.

> *We work to the same methodology, we use the same language, we meet regularly, we share information, but we challenge risk management. We challenge their methodology, we challenge their performance, we challenge their rate of progress, but yet, you know, we work very closely.* (Q)

Some respondents considered box 4 would be a very unusual situation. The companies of those placing themselves there had no common features. One was experiencing significant organisational change as a result of a demerger and was in the process of bringing an outsourced internal audit function in-house, after which the interviewee confidently expected the company to be moving towards closer integration, a box 2 position. The pressure for this change was self-induced: the head of internal audit had strong views on the internal audit role in the organisation. Another in box 4 was a smaller company with no formal internal audit function. Traditional compliance auditing was undertaken on a limited basis by finance staff and external consultants were employed to provide assurance for the board on Turnbull compliance. No change was anticipated. The third company in box 4 had only recently introduced a formal internal audit function and this was currently viewed as "bolt-on": future integration was possible but vague in outline. In the fourth company in box 4, the risk management system was a well-established corporate process from which a traditional internal audit function was quite detached.

Those in box 3 described stable positions. In one company, a long-standing head of internal audit had recently retired: his replacement had joined from a larger, more risk-oriented company but did not indicate that he would be initiating change to the compliance-based system he had inherited, although he described himself as a risk manager. In the other company in box 3, internal audit had been viewed as too risk-based and the current head had been requested by the board on his appointment to return to a more traditional approach.

The characterisation of box 1 as internal audit keen to colonise other risk areas was only part of the picture presented by these interviewees, since this might be just one facet of the drive by internal audit to move the company to a more holistic approach to risk management, an ambition shared by all in this box who expected to move to a box 2 position.

Summary

In summary, an overall dynamic of movement towards the top right-hand corner of the matrix could be discerned. The main driver of this movement appeared to be an individual or group who were championing change: for example, the appointment of a chairman or chief executive or a head of internal audit with a particular vision of the role. Organisational change, benchmarking and the implementation of Turnbull were all used by such champions as opportunities to win hearts and minds. The aspiration towards integration of internal audit with risk management is understandable if internal auditors want to secure their corporate position, especially where risk management is seen as a vital component of strategic and operational decisions, whereas internal control may be perceived as more peripheral. This dynamic is one aspect of the changes in internal audit which form a common thread running through the responses of the interviewees.

The analysis in this chapter provides confirmation of the aspirations of internal auditors towards integration of their role with risk management, as highlighted in the literature discussed previously, and some indication of the extent to which this has been achieved. It also offers more detail of the organisational context in which this aspiration is set and identifies some of the drivers of this ongoing development. It further demonstrates the need to consider the impact of organisational change and the internal audit's role in that process. These issues are developed further in chapters five and six in which the interview data was analysed using a grounded theory approach.

ENDNOTE:

---

[1] The positions of T and U are inferred from interview data.

Chapter Five

The Turnbull Report,
Internal Audit and Risk Management

This chapter deals with the impact of the Turnbull Report on the work of the interviewees and their companies and explores the ways in which the companies identified and managed risk. The discussion is presented under headings based on the broad areas of the research questions identified earlier. Each heading is supported by a series of grids (tables) containing concepts, categories and dimensions identified in the analysis (see Appendix Two).

The grids were constructed as the final part of the process of analysis of the transcripts and notes of the interviews. Each grid is in three columns. The first column contains selective codings of the concepts which were expressed in the interviews. Some of these concepts summarise the thoughts that were expressed by several interviewees, others reflect the flavour of only one set of comments. The rows of the grids group concepts into categories and the final column contains the dimensions of variation within the categories. The dimensions are either expressed as end points of a continuum (*eg* 'IA centralised *vs* IA decentralised') or as variables which can vary from zero upwards (*eg* 'Speed of response', 'extent of use of risk based methods', 'extent of horizontal communication'). Sometimes a single expression is used to express more than one dimension (*eg* 'Seniority and diversity'). Each of the grids is headed with an overall category descriptor.

Eleven grids are discussed in this chapter, as follows:

- Turnbull and Turnbull disclosures (Grids 1 and 2)

- Risk identification, assessment and management (Grid 3)

- Organisation of internal audit and its current role (Grids 4, 5, 6 and 7)

- The crystallisation of risks, relationships and engagement with boards and audit committees and other risk functions (Grids 8, 9 and 10)

- Involvement of internal audit in strategy (Grid 11)

Turnbull and Turnbull disclosures (Grids 1 and 2)

One impact of Turnbull was the need to consider the route by which the board obtained assurance about risk management. Where there was specific reporting on risk to a risk committee, assurance was provided as part of the process; where risk was 'just another management function' an alternative needed to be found (such as internal audit reporting). Methods adopted to achieve this are discussed in more detail under the next heading "Risk identification, assessment and management".

The introduction of the Turnbull guidance gave internal audit departments a new training role. In some cases this involved a significant shift in approach:

> So we gave everybody within internal audit a one day training course … The key phrase was 'think risk then control' because, of course, auditors previously had always been focused on controls and we were trying to get them to think slightly differently now, but think risk and then control. … Whereas it used to be you go and interview somebody and say "Right, what controls have you got to ensure that X gets paid Y amount on the date", whereas now you would go in and say "What are the risks to you achieving your objectives for this particular job?" and that is where they would start from. So that was

quite key, so we literally undertook a whole programme of training for everybody to do that, and we also backed it up with a computer based training package so that people could go back and get the messages reinforced. We changed our opinions in our audit reports to focus on risks rather than control, we changed some of the templates in our audit reports so again, so we weren't looking at internal controls, it was that we were looking at risks, you know, and so on and so forth. So we did quite a step change, really. (M)

However, most interviewees indicated that the main impact of the need to comply with Turnbull disclosure requirements had been a formalisation of pre-existing procedures. The following three interviewees illuminate this point:

So, for example, when, with the risk analysis that the company secretary does on an annual basis, until Turnbull came in, that had never been done on such a formal basis, so we'd never written down what we thought what are the 25 biggest risks to the business. That had never been written down in any one place, but it was implicit in a lot of what we did, but it had never been formalised and co-ordinated in that way. So, I think its made us focus on having a more definite list and trying to think if there are any gaps, any weaknesses we need to address. (C)

Turnbull came along roughly at the same time as we became a plc, so this is what we've been doing almost from day one. As part of creating this plc environment to work in ... We have been quite lucky because it has made it quite a simple process. We've put things in and from the management's point of view we've formalised the process that was going on in the background, but never documented. (I)

I think that the level of awareness and impact was very clear, but remember that because their philosophy and approach within company K was focused on risk management, really we just needed to make sure that the demonstration of that was effective. There wasn't a sudden "Oh gee, we had better introduce risk management into this organisation", I mean it was just the recognition of "Is our robustness and documentation around it clear?" as opposed to a philosophy and intent process, that type of thing. So it was definitely much more of "As a business are we in a position to demonstrate that we are already doing it?" (S)

But in other companies the impact had been greater:

Turnbull coming in really did shake us up and it shook the bigwigs up in the fact that it wasn't something you could ignore, which I think is absolutely right. (P)

The formalisation of procedures required by Turnbull compliance could be seen as beneficial:

... for a small plc like ourselves, I think our consolidated view is that Turnbull is a necessary evil rather than it being "Oh my gosh, isn't this bringing us something particularly new and valuable to the way we run our business". That's our corporate view ... we try to make it work for us as best we can and at least extract what value we can from it ... what Turnbull forces us to do is to, again, spend time with each business and well, what it should be is that they write down and assess and quantify the risks that each business feels that it faces. That kind of management review system ... was around long before Turnbull was around. I think what is interesting is some of the guys down at business unit level, take it more seriously than others and I think, there are certainly a number of the guys who actually use the exercise as an opportunity to talk through risks with their own management team, and to that extent, that's quite a useful exercise. And you can see it in the quality of what comes back. (D)

More negative views suggested Turnbull was only a 'compliance thing' or that 'assurance was the only added bit' or that it was a 'necessary evil for small plcs'.

In general, however, the changes were seen as positive. As well as formalisation of processes, in some businesses, Turnbull was seen as strengthening risk management, for example in various ways, such as non-financial controls or easing the introduction of Control Risk Self Assessment. It was also seen as improving the standing of internal audit and communication with divisional managers.

> *... the Turnbull Report came in slightly before I joined, but we knew we had to bring it on board. It is probably ... on the non-financial side, it's just sort of strengthened us, looking at that and not just the financial side for internal audit. (O)*

> *We could see which way the wind was blowing and I was already steering my team in that direction, so that we were prepared. What we then had to do when the final guidance came out was to move the whole organisation. A number of us could see what needed to be done, but it did require some sensitive organisational changes, so we got ... our external auditors ... to do a quick study of our corporate governance arrangements. Effectively to tell us what we knew needed to be done anyway, but it legitimised it. (Q)*

Normally, internal auditors, finance directors, company secretaries and other senior managers with a risk management brief would be involved in drafting the statement on the effectiveness of internal control for approval by the audit committee and the board. One company with no internal audit function employed consultants to do this.

> *... to take some of the workload off me, I've actually employed some external risk consultants ... We scope out an exercise, they go and do some of the visits, they crank up the software, cajole people along,*

just project manage it, if you like … they will propose wording and I'll fiddle about with it a bit, and that's how we end up with the wording that we've got in our annual report. (D)

Examining the published reports of the companies also reveal a wide range of approaches. At one end of the spectrum is a very brief statement that long-established risk management procedures are in place, coupled with an acknowledgement of directors' responsibility; in contrast lie lengthy descriptions of the internal control framework and risk-management process, sometimes with an outline of some of the specific risks faced by the company.

(We) disclosed the whole risk-management process. I felt we were being honest with the shareholders as to where we were with the process. (P)

Several interviewees mentioned that the Turnbull Report was not the only force for internal control and risk management disclosure. In particular, the requirements for US listing and the interest of investors were given priority over Turnbull as determinants of disclosures by individual interviewees. One interviewee commented that institutional investors were increasingly interested in social and environmental reporting, rather than Turnbull disclosures.

Risk identification, assessment and management (Grid 3)

The involvement of internal audit with risk management varies from a distant review of process to being intimately bound up with it. Respondents' descriptions of the risk identification, assessment and management processes in their organisations provide some insights into the forces driving the dynamic identified in the matrix in chapter four.

Formalised risk-management procedures were at various stages of implementation, although most interviewees felt that effective risk management was already in place prior to Turnbull. The Turnbull requirements were generally viewed as helpful in formalising existing processes and providing opportunities for internal audit to link more closely to audit committees and to other organisational areas where risk issues were already being addressed. Interviewees spoke of co-operation with insurance managers and company secretaries in raising awareness of the need to establish formal processes.

Post Turnbull, risk management committees existed in several companies. These committees were sub-committees of the board in each case and had representatives from operating units as well. Typically the committees received reports from operating units and maintained a group risk register. Some companies devolved risk to operating units in the same way as other management responsibilities, others maintained parallel reporting of risk to the risk committee. Risk registers were to be found in both systems – either maintained centrally or at divisions or business units. Where divisions maintained risk registers there was a need to check that they were properly updated; this was managed through risk committee meetings or by the use of interactive software.

Anybody, anywhere in the business, at any time of day or night can notify a new risk into the risk constellation. (V)

The process of risk-identification involved internal audit in various ways, from consultation at a senior level:

… we did an exercise which was just the internal audit manager, myself and the finance director. We sat down and we actually each did it independently, we went through the companies we have got and then picked various drivers. (O)

- to facilitation of workshops:

I got the board of each business together (the top 20 people), and talked about risk. Of course, the reactions ranged from "This is bureaucratic and why do we have to do this?" to "This is interesting". So what I did was hold a facilitated workshop with each of the business and the major corporate functions and got them to produce their top risks, whatever they came up with, in some cases it was 50 or 60, but at least a top 20, rated by financial impact, reputational impact and the likelihood of occurrence. So we had all this massive amount of input and I wanted to put something to the board that perhaps we could talk about the top ten risks to the group. So the question was how to go from all these hundreds of risks input to the top ten for the group. (B)

We had a massive programme of what we call deep-dives, which was an American technique … it's like a variant on brain storming. … And it's done in every area, legal, technology, finance, every headquarter area did one, treasury, operations, customer care, procurement. Gradually, from these roots it eventually works its way up to the board … It's all very bottom up. (V)

Ensuring completeness of risk–identification is a potential problem and companies had a range of solutions. Approaches included: examining the different risks at each stage of the value chain; checking against an inventory of different possible risks; examining the organisation function by function, process by process or business unit by business unit; Control Risk Self Assessment techniques; and proprietary software. The most popular method for effecting these approaches was by means of workshops.

The processes of risk–identification and assessment were often combined, especially where workshops were used:

… we sat down with a cross-section of every function, making sure we had as many people as possible involved, and we just went and sat and talked through every process that we actually performed

within that area. We sat and thought about whether there were risks associated at every stage within the process and we documented that process down, and then we graded the risk; basically, the likelihood of the problem occurring, the risk occurring and the impact it would have if it did. We have risks that are red, that are amber, that are green – if we are sitting in the green area then we are comfortable with it. If it's in amber we should have an action plan, but it's not as serious as it could be. If it's in red we had to have an action plan and an implementation date to make sure we were coming at least into amber, if not into the green. (I)

… we use an anonymous voting technology in the workshops, so first of all we identify the risks to the achievement of their objective, and then the risks are discussed to make sure everybody understands what the risk is, so we don't have risks that just say "People". It has to be a specific issue, so we get that first so that everybody understands the risk. Then we vote on the impact of the risk on the achievement of the objectives and the likelihood of the risk coming to fruition, and at this stage we are looking at gross risk, so what we are saying to them is, we want you to have on the table all the risks that could happen, regardless of how well you think that you are managing them. So, they may be a risk to business continuity, for example, if something happens to the building or the power, but they may know or they may think that they have got it covered, because they have got backup generators, and they have got a building they can move into, so they may not see that as a risk, because they have got all the other things in place, so we tell them to try and forget what they have got in place and put everything down. So when we are voting on impact and likelihood we are voting on both those criteria as if there was nothing in place. So what you end up with is a list of prioritised risks, some of which may be managed very, very well, but they are prioritised risks regardless of what is being done about them. (M)

Workshops are discussed in more detail under the heading "Communication" in chapter six.

In some companies, risk assessment was formalised using heuristic devices developed within internal audit:

> *What we've found subsequently was the little technique of having a little brainstorming session was being used throughout. Because you'd go to talk to somebody about a new project, say, and out would come the little 3by3, and people were automatically doing it. So it really was getting embedded as a mechanism, which was extremely gratifying and also proved that it works as a business tool, which was very helpful.* (A)

Risk assessment was sometimes carried out using software that internal audit either used directly or trained managers to use.

> *We go to each business unit with a format … we've bought in a little software tool, which is a tailored questionnaire which kind of gets you thinking about risks in a generic, fairly standard way, but allows you to add new risks, delete risks that aren't appropriate, so over time you end up with something which is reasonably appropriate to each business unit and then it's a case of sitting down with each managing director of each of those business units and just going through this whole process of these are the risks that we think that we've identified, how do those rank in terms of impact, what is the likelihood … the classic taking you through the Turnbull bit. So we end up with a document for each business unit, which summarises their risk profile.* (D)

The assessment of risks was carried out using various models. Implicit in most of the models was an expected-value framework in which risks were measured as the product of their expected impact and the probability of their occurrence. Companies also attempted to assess the probability of a risk occurring without the company's controls in place and then to assess the probability given the existing controls. While this seems a reasonable way to proceed in many instances, the impacts of many risks are difficult to quantify and human judgements of probability are notoriously error prone. Moreover risks are rarely uncorrelated so one adverse event is likely to increase the probability of others occurring. These problems are further compounded by the filtering of risks which takes place. Risk workshops came up with large numbers of risks and companies decided to concentrate on only a few of them.

> *When it comes to reporting it to the main board, they don't want to hear about 300 risks, they want to hear about 30 of them, so that's how we arranged it.* (P)

The problem with cutting out risks which are adjudged of low probability is that there are a lot of them; it is quite likely that some of the low probability high impact risks will happen. However, none of the interviewees seemed conscious of this as a problem.

Risk assessment was summarised in various ways. In some companies a three by three matrix of high, medium and low impact by high, medium and low probability was used. Risks which were high impact and high probability were the ones which were prioritised. Other variants of this were to give risks a numerical score between, say, 1 and 20 or a 'traffic light' system in which prioritised risks were red lights and so on. (Low, medium and high risks were pithily described by one of the respondents as "Oh, well", "Oh, dear", and "Oh, shit".) Overlaying the risk assessment were elements of judgement and higher authority which could change the priorities of risks.

Risks were recorded in risk registers (also described as "risk logs", "risk bibles", "the risk universe", "the risk constellation").

> *… each of the key parts of the business performs a control risk self assessment workshop that we facilitate, which helps them to identify the key risks to the achievement of their objectives for that business*

unit or business division. From that they produce a risk register. The risks that are identified at the workshop may not be a full list of risks because there may be other things that they need to take into account, but the risk workshop kicks that process off. (M)

Compiling, reviewing and maintaining these records would form a part of the activities of risk committees, operational committees at central group or business unit level. Internal audit involvement with risk committees varied from directly influencing their establishment:

I formed the Group Risk Committee. I asked our head of strategy, who was part of our executive management team and thus carried a lot of authority, to chair it … if anything, what we're talking about is risk to achieving a group strategy. So it would be most appropriate to have the head of strategy there to relate and to keep bringing us back to well, it maybe a risk, but strategically, its not very important. (B)

– to participation:

… internal audit are on the risk management group and on the risk management committee, and obviously attend the audit committee meetings. (I)

– to observation:

So in terms of our role within risk assessment and risk management I would say it is very much that we are an observer of the risk committee. (H)

Risk committees varied in their constitution and activity. In some cases they generated the internal audit programme, in others they initiated specific projects:

… somebody within the risk committee … will actually be assigned, OK you are now the risk champion for this particular area, we need

to go away and we need to ensure that, you know, controls around preventing business espionage are adequate or whatever. (H)

Interviewees often talked about these processes of identifying and assessing risks in terms of embedding risk awareness within the organisational culture.

So it is really trying to ensure there is a risk aware culture within the whole business and that everybody thinks risk, because anyone that is a manager in the business should be a risk manager really. (H)

In some companies, the process of risk identification and assessment was less sophisticated:

It's my judgement, I guess. Judgement and experience, I think is probably the only thing. There are no hard and fast rules in terms of it. So it really comes down to my assessment of how weak ... a particular area is and how important to the business that particular area is. That takes into account a number of factors which will include materiality, an assessment of management, the environment in which they operate, past experience does have a fairly high priority within that assessment ... My view has always been that a highly sophisticated approach to risk assessment, to be quite honest, is not necessarily wholly appropriate. (J)

Some interviewees had risk assessment and identification processes in place but acknowledged that they could be improved:

The new MD is particularly keen on looking at the risk management process, because I don't think it is quite there yet. I think we know the risks but I think it is just needs to be smartened up. (O)

We have, in theory, risk management committees within each country, but I think that process needs to be re-energised, if you like. (K)

The relationship between internal audit and the risk management process varied between companies and was evolving in response to organisational and other changes:

> *[Internal audit] is integrated with the whole concept of risk management, but organisationally it is not part of the risk management function. You know, we made the decision and have reassessed that decision and reaffirmed it, to keep the two functions separate. That risk management is part of management assurance and internal audit should be communicating totally with the risk management function, but has to be independent. We work to the same methodology, we use the same language, we meet regularly, we share information, but we challenge risk management. We challenge their methodology, we challenge their performance, we challenge their rate of progress, but yet, you know, we work very closely. I don't know what you have found but I find more and more companies are actually going that way in the UK and in Europe. There's quite a few started with an integrated audit and risk management function, the sort of fuzzy solution, and more and more companies are now separating them out. (Q)*

Organisation of internal audit and its current role (Grids 4, 5, 6 and 7)

Organisation of internal audit (Grid 4)

One of the surprising findings of the research is the diversity of arrangements for organising internal audit. In some organisations there were dedicated internal audit departments which only undertook auditing. In others, internal audit was combined with process review, in which the department had a specific brief for the analysis and modification of business process and systems in different parts of the organisation. In some cases the internal audit role was explicitly linked to risk management:

> ... a lot of internal audits now are calling themselves "internal audit and business risk" or "risk and internal audit" ... a lot of them are combined now. (M)

In most companies internal audit was centralised but where the function was decentralised it reported to divisional management, rather than through the Head of Internal Audit. In some cases, central internal audit had no apparent control over these divisional functions. In some companies internal audit was carried out on a peer review basis or by members of the finance staff in a 'part-time' capacity.

The authors asked to whom internal audit reported. The prevalent description was that internal audit reported to the financial director, but had a 'dotted line' reporting responsibility to the audit committee. Two organisations were actively considering changing the reporting line so that internal audit would report directly to the audit committee. In all cases the head of internal audit attended audit committee meetings and internal audit reports were made available to the audit committee.

The interviewees expressed subtly different perspectives on what internal audit was doing. Internal audit was described as focusing on risk management, or being 'all about risk and control', and the departments were variously auditing processes, or controls, or compliance.

Auditors saw themselves as providing 'comfort' and 'assurance' to divisional managers and the board that controls were working and systems were reliable, as well as making recommendations for improved processes. None of the interviewees explicitly expressed the view that they were part of a monitoring process which, by providing the threat of discovery, helped to reduce the prevalence of error or fraud. By conducting investigations and reviews, departments also provided management with information.

The extent of this variation does not seem to be strongly linked to contextual variables such as company size or the nature of the business. It may also be symptomatic of the endemic nature of change in businesses that a single model of internal audit has not become widespread.

Outsourcing (Grid 5)

During the 1980s, the analysis of the contribution of central corporate services through the application of business process re-engineering techniques, suggested that, in some circumstances, cost savings could be made by contracting out functions such as payroll, information technology and internal audit. This offered a business opportunity for the large accountancy firms and led to pressure on existing internal audit departments to show how their activities added value.

Companies which outsource internal audit still need a nominal head of internal audit, a senior manager with responsibility for liaison with the outsource provider, but the role will be rather different from that of a head of internal audit who leads a team of staff employed by the company.

Only two of the companies examined had a fully outsourced internal audit function. Another had reverted from outsourcing in the recent past while yet another was in the process of re-establishing an in-house team due to dissatisfaction with the outsourced service received. Co-sourcing arrangements varied, from extensive external provision in one company, where an in-house internal auditor led teams from an outsource provider on international audit assignments, to another where only information systems audits were undertaken by an external provider. "Topping up" arrangements involved buying in specific skills where necessary, such as treasury or information systems expertise which might not be available within the company.

One company had bought in a specifically tailored investigation of Turnbull compliance which included the drafting of the Turnbull disclosure statement by the external provider. In several companies the possibility of outsourcing was kept under regular review. The interviewees expressed well-rehearsed arguments about its advantages and disadvantages.

One company which currently outsourced its internal audit had done so because it was perceived as the best way of making a rapid change in the nature of the internal audit function. Over time, changes in the company and the redeployment of managers without a finance background to internal audit had changed the internal audit function into an *ad hoc* consultancy provider. Concern at board level about the high costs and the lack of focus on financial controls led to the appointment of a new head of internal audit who investigated the views of management within the group's companies as to what they wanted from internal audit. The response indicated a need for a more traditional approach:

> ... *there was a fairly consistent answer that, first and foremost, they wanted to be able to sleep at night, they wanted to know that the basic control processes were in place. They all acknowledged that there's more to internal audit than that, but because that hadn't been looked at for so long, probably four or five years, that was what they wanted.* (B)

Outsourcing offered a speedier and cheaper solution than disbanding the current function and appointing a new in-house team. The group was large enough to command a dedicated team from the outsource provider:

> *They are not known as [outsource provider] here, they're known as GIA - Group Internal Audit. They look like, and sound like, employees.* (B)

The second company which had outsourced internal audit had been recently demerged from a group which had outsourced finance, IT and internal audit at the same time in the mid 1990s. Although the outsourcing arrangement was regularly reviewed, the company was considered too small to retain a cost-effective in-house internal audit function.

The company that had abandoned outsourcing had very specific reasons for the change. Internal audit had been outsourced to the company's external auditors at the time of the company's de-merger from a larger group before the appointment of the current group financial controller. He was dissatisfied with the service provided:

It's useful paying for the expertise for the sort of planning and reviewing at the end but the actual doing of it can actually be done by more junior and less expensive people to actually go out on site … we weren't getting enough in the way of actionable recommendations. So it would be very traditional internal audit recommendations along the lines of 'You were doing this, this is wrong', recommendation 'Do it better', as opposed to 'How about trying this?' (C)

He had also expected some sharing of best practice from the outsource provider's experience with other clients, or even within the group companies:

… we were pretty de-centralised upon de-merger and different practices were prevalent in different sites and we never got to grips with, if there was best practice in one site, to make sure that that was replicated across the whole piece. (C)

Arguments cited against outsourcing were: cost, inflexibility, lack of employee loyalty, lack of detailed understanding of the business, value of having people on the premises and available for consultation, probable sales pressure from the internal audit provider and the loss of the value of internal audit as a training ground for employees. The following comments illustrate these views:

> *I think the issue is they tend to always look at it as an external auditor. Even though you give them the programme, they have a mentality that is external audit. They don't even necessarily get to understand individual businesses.* (J)

> *We want a core internal audit function who knows the business and [will] be loyal to our business, because they're our employees. We don't want a firm of outside accountants doing it when the manager on the job is aware that the more fee he can sell us, the more brownie points he gets towards his partnership goal. That was also quite clearly expressed that we don't want to let a load of salesmen in – that we really don't want because we have enough trouble with the external auditors without internal auditors doing it too.* (A)

> *… to outsource and get understanding and value for money would be very difficult.* (P)

> *I am fundamentally opposed to outsourcing internal audit unless the internal audit gets so small because the business is so small that it can't sort of have the breadth and development of its people that an audit function should have.* (F)

Outsourcing providers were also perceived as 'too financial accounting oriented' and to view the work 'as an external auditor'.

Size was an important factor in outsourcing decisions: it was viewed as appropriate for smaller companies where a cost-effective in-house team could not be sustained. As stated above, a form of internal peer review, possibly with some external purchase of specialist skills was another means of providing a fundamental internal audit function, although it was recognised that the Turnbull requirements might force a greater formalisation of this provision.

The interviewees did not view outsourcing as a general threat to the status of internal audit. Decisions on outsourcing had either been driven by, or taken in consultation with, internal audit. Although they expressed a range of views, based on their own previous experience, as to its benefits, there was a general recognition that its value would be determined by specific company circumstances which would vary over time and that it could, with advantage, be partially implemented by co-sourcing and topping up.

Composition of internal audit teams (Grid 6)

The picture of internal audit departments provided by the interviewees is one of more or less continuous staff change. Most of the heads of internal audit interviewed had been in post for three years or less. Some had moved from a similar post in another company, others had been appointed, or had internal audit responsibilities added to their remit, during recent organisational changes.

The expectation was that their staff would remain for an average of two years, often moving on to other posts within the company/group.

> *I think the role is pretty demanding in terms of the requirements for them to be away from their homes and to travel is quite tiring, and my experience has been that the moment people get towards three years, to be quite honest, they've had enough. They may not actually realise that they've had enough, but they have. (J)*

The size of audit teams varied between one (where internal audit was outsourced) and eighty-five (a company which also provided internal audit services to other companies which had demerged from its main group), although most teams were about six strong. The background and qualifications of team members was predominantly financial, although this varied, especially where internal audit provided an acknowledged training function and brought in staff from other parts of the company. This very significant aspect of internal audit activity and its implications are discussed in more detail under 'Education and Development' in chapter six.

Some of the interviewees highlighted a need for specific skills in the audit team, most often relating to IT. Where necessary, such specialists were brought in from other parts of the organisation or through outsourcing. In some cases the move to a risk perspective on internal audit had driven this requirement:

> *We've actually brought in from the business a guy that is a civil engineer by trade and in his time with the construction company he was very involved in risk management, that type of stuff.* (S)

> *What we saw with Turnbull was an opportunity to create jobs for experts from the business. Because if you're looking at broad business risk, you're going to start looking into areas where your team of largely accountants, really haven't got the right skill base.* (A)

However, views on the need for specialist skills varied widely:

> *… you don't have to be a clown to audit a circus.* (Q)

One company with a large branch structure had a 'core compliance' team of internal auditors who were largely unqualified staff carrying out branch audits. The work of these staff was contrasted with 'corporate' audits done by the remainder of the department.

Negotiation of audit plan (Grid 7)

Where a formal risk-assessment process was well-established, the internal audit work programme was often closely linked to this and usually consisted of testing of the controls which management relied upon for assurance. However this was not universal. Some companies which rated themselves as high on a risk-based auditing approach nevertheless said that their work plan was not explicitly linked to formal risk assessment and was derived from rotation and judgement.

If areas of concern had been identified, it might be necessary to drill down using a traditional compliance audit but, generally, line management was seen as carrying the responsibility for compliance and internal audit's role should be to test the process used, rather than to repeat it. In some companies internal audit was responsive to the stated needs of business units – where they required core financial assurance, this would be provided through a traditional 'tick and bash' audit process.

Several companies operated a three to five year rolling plan which focused on specific business areas each year – for example, customer service departments in year one, followed by health and safety and environmental issues in year two and support services such as IT in year three. Others based the cycle on the results of risk assessment:

> *In essence, we risk-rate all our businesses around the world, essentially high, medium and low risk. And that determines, if you like, a basic audit cycle, which is every year for high risk, every two years for medium risk and every three years for low risk. (J)*

Against this background, an annual work programme was often determined by a dual approach which married issues arising from the risk-management process with those flagged up directly by internal audit itself on the basis of prior experience and discussions with business units.

> *We have a risk-based approach to auditing in that we have a universe of every entity that we could audit and that is assessed on a risk score and from that universe we strip off the jobs with the highest risk score to include in our plan of work. But as well as that we look at the risk registers that the lines of business hold and make sure that we cover everything that they have identified as key. ... We make our own decisions on what we think we should be auditing and then we*

compare that with what the business says are their key risks to make sure that we have covered them from both angles. The reason for that is that potentially management could miss a risk and indeed so could we if we just used ours so we look at the two together. (M)

So basically, we'll take every area and go through and say what's new, what's happening, what's changed, where have we had problems before and allocate some time along those heading from there. So that's done at a high level with myself and the audit manager. The audit manager then goes round to each of the line directors and discusses the proposed plan with them, and if they want to tweak it, they want to look in any other direction that needs to come through. So that plan will then get tweaked accordingly with more emphasis on other areas, and with what their needs might be and that plan is finalised and put to the audit committee for approval. The risk management group meets on a bi-monthly basis ... and we sit down and go through the work programme to make sure that anything that's started has been completed properly. New risks are identified and tabled by each area at that meeting and actions are decided on as to what we will be doing about that risk. (I)

The programme was usually agreed with the audit committee. Some were more proactive than others:

... we negotiate the audits we're going to do with the audit committee – I mean basically we propose what we're going to do and they approve it – but its also worked in conjunction with the head of risk management and the FD to make sure we're looking at the right area. ... Occasionally the audit committee will ask us to look at something specific. (P)

Formal programmes might be agreed with the audit committee for a year in advance but in practice this would change, often at short notice:

The audit committee agree our plan of work for the twelve months and the client agrees our plan of work for twelve months, and then what happens is the audit committee or the group finance director or the CEO will say "I want this investigated"... and it won't be in the plan of work. So then we have got an inject, that's an injected job. So then the plan has to be juggled to incorporate that work, which actually may be of a lower risk than some of the work that we have already got in there, but if the CEO says I want this looked at, then we look at it, or if the board audit committee want it looked at then we would look at it. So the plan is agreed, the twelve month plan is agreed with the board audit committee and the client, but it can change and in ... today's world it will change ... you can bet your life that it will change. (M)

Where no formal internal audit function was in place, a process of peer review between business units was sometimes used but interviewees expressed doubts about whether this could provide adequate Turnbull assurance.

Assistance was provided to the external auditors where it could be factored into the work programme without distorting it, in some companies. For the most part, however, relations with external audit were distant:

... in terms of financial matters, they can place some reliance on the work we do ... obviously one of the things they do is look through our files and at least we've recorded the fact that Joe Bloggs has done his bank reconciliation at least at the times of the year that we have visited. So I guess they gain some comfort from that and, of course, we always have an interesting debate about whether that means the fees are going to come down or not, but it never seems to be quite enough. (D)

The crystallisation of risks, relationships and engagement with boards and audit committees and other risk functions (Grids 8, 9 and 10)

Crystallisation of risks (Grid 8)

There was no common expression to describe a risk that had occurred, although in one company thought had been given to the language used:

> *Yes, we did have a long debate about what the word was for when you identify a risk with a likelihood and impact. When a risk happens, what do you call it? I don't know why, we came up with crystallising ... But I know we did have huge debates about what the word was. We had risks occurring, but we felt that didn't feel right. Because something happens, doesn't mean it's necessarily bad, it just happens. So we thought it's all about crystallising. Over here, we've got a hypothetical situation, if you like, and it hardens on you, so we ended up with crystallising. (A)*

The types of risk identified and their likelihood and impact varied enormously within and among companies. Interviewees described events that, although unanticipated, were dealt with by well-established emergency responses and standard business continuity procedures:

> *We have what's called emergency response, which we are required to have, and for example 11 September we did have to invoke emergency response ... These meeting rooms here are actually put aside, they cleared out their set-up for emergency response quickly and the directors can then decide what actions need to be taken, do we need to be manning phones all night ... The risk committee would then review at the next committee following on from something such as an event that has required emergency response to be invoked. It would*

then review what had happened and well, where we have identified this risk on our matrix. (H)

Reactions to risk crystallisation varied:

We have set procedures if something goes wrong. We capture the information, it is reported, it is evaluated, we have got targets. (S)

Any new occurrence is reported to the board at the next board meeting. If it's an occurrence of any magnitude … we've got a direct link into the board via the committee sponsor who's the chief operating officer. But for the smaller things, if there is an occurrence of a risk of a lower level that's not actually a significant risk, then it is reported to me, we talk about another occurrence of it, whether it was a particular type of fraud we've discovered or things like that, then we would work with regional operations to try and plug that gap or do an audit in that area … We would react to it, put it that way. (P)

Some interviewees emphasised the importance of learning from the incident:

Last year in one of our businesses, there was a major shift in raw material prices. They didn't respond with market sales price adjustments quickly enough, and consequently, it took quite a financial hit. I pointed out to them that they had in fact forecast that this was going to be a major risk, but they hadn't actually followed their own advice and got it right. Which they acknowledged and immediately tightened up their own process, which they had thought would work but didn't work quickly enough. That gets spread around the group as a case of a good example. You can't just pay lip service to these so called controls – it's got to be real, otherwise it will cost you money. We don't want to be sitting here in hindsight saying we knew that was a risk and we failed to take care of it. Shutting stable doors afterwards is not what we want to be doing. We try to shut the stable door up front. (B)

We had a risk crystallise in [group company], a major risk crystallise – their major supplier in the US went into Chapter 11 – so, of course, everyone was scurrying back "Was it on the risk matrix?" And it was there – it wasn't high, but it was there. They looked at it and said we've identified it, so these are the controls, so why didn't we spot it coming? Is there anything we could have done differently? So they found they could actually use it to key in on "Well, we did that, we did that, maybe we could have done this better". One of the things they found and fed back to everyone else, was actually they hadn't documented the controls very well, because there was, in fact, more that they did around it, than they'd actually put down. But, if they'd put it down, they might have spotted that actually that one isn't working, and they weren't getting nearly enough warning. So, very quickly, we had a scenario where it actually became a living, working document and people were able to see the use of it. And that helped hugely, of course, because as soon as you've actually used it in anger, then everybody thinks, 'Cor blimey, I'd better check mine to see if it works'. (A)

In one example, a newly established risk committee was found to be very helpful:

We've gone through the process with the police, health and safety executive, [local council], all the controls through this committee to see what we'd been doing, what we'd done in terms of maintenance, whether it was our responsibility, the contractors, whether it was pure accident, all that kind of stuff. We've worked through that whole process with the risk management committee, following through what's been happening … So the risk management committee takes over in the event of a major disaster and works through the process and controls the process of finding out what's happening and taking remedial action and taking longer term action to sort these things out.

[It was] the first time the risk management committee has had to do anything significant at all. And it's worked very well. (I)

Relationships and engagement with boards and audit committees (Grid 9)

In two companies, the board had taken an active interest in refocusing internal audit on core assurance activities, moving away from more risk-centred and consultancy approaches:

Because of the acquisition problems they had in the mid-90s, they were a bit unhappy that there wasn't enough review going on. (E)

... internal audit ... had lost credibility, it did not appear to have the capabilities to do what the businesses wanted it to do ... First and foremost, they wanted to be able to sleep at night, they wanted to know that the basic control processes were in place. (B)

In most companies the relationship between internal audit and the board was mediated *via* the audit committee. Audit committees varied in their interest and involvement with internal audit, from the minimum level of rubber-stamping the work programme to a more proactive stance. The latter was generally much appreciated by internal auditors:

I actually think it is brilliant in comparison to the previous audit committee, where I think I, as the head of audit of one particular division, I was seen once by that committee and it was a very big committee, loads of people on it, it seemed, but I have got a very focused audit committee with three non-execs. The CFO and I turn up, and the external auditors. We meet formally once a quarter and each quarter there is a set agenda of what we are going to review. It is very much a two way thing and [audit committee chair] and I will present the findings from that quarter for example and the audit committee will then request that I follow particular things up or that I do, or we do some kind of work on some particular area.

So, yes, we have got a very interested audit committee and [audit committee chair] is obviously very active as well, and will go out and meet with our risk managers, then contact me and say "can you have a look at ...". [Audit committee chair] is actually very interested and that's great because it makes you feel like what you are doing is actually being taken notice of and is worthwhile, so it is quite nice actually. (H)

There has been a slight change in that we've had a new audit committee chairman and in some ways he is a bit more demanding. He asks for updates on specific issues that have been dealt with at an audit committee between the audit committee meetings. The previous one never did. (J)

Some interviewees had very clear ideas of how the audit committee should work and their own relationship to it:

And one of the things that I've been quite clear about, in the audit committee's remit, only put in place in the audit committee's charter since I've been here, the audit committee is responsible for assessing the process, which is being used to identify managed risks. They are not responsible for telling them what the risks are. The board are responsible for identifying key business risks. To me, the way I interpret Turnbull ... the board will need to form its own view, the role of board committees, including the audit committee, is for the board to decide ... So it says quite clearly that the audit committee can review the process but not challenge the risk. (F)

A key task of internal audit was to assist the audit committee:

I think largely our job in this regard is to make sure the process of identifying the risk and the control round it is a good one, so that the audit committee can consider that risk and can invite any of the businesses to come in and talk about those risks in relation to their business, or just sit there and talk to the CEO and CFO about the risk. Which they do. I think, if I can help ensure that what the committee sees is a list produced from a thorough and comprehensive and reasonably frequent review process, then that gives them some comfort. They don't look to me for assurance that the risk has been eliminated. (B)

And we actually brought that alive for the audit committee so that they could actually understand how internal control is then embedded into business. You know, it is not a tick and a bash thing or whatever, it is either in there or it is not. So we wanted to show them that so that the audit committee could form a view of what the management team is telling it over how it is managing its business. (S)

Some interviewees found the relationship problematic:

I actually went to the audit committee and said "I am concerned that in being less than a year in U I have seen issues of health and safety and environment, issues of fraud, coming up in the group and I am not sure we are really committed. We say that U is a service company, the essence of U is service in integrity and we have got a lot of notices about that, but I don't think that has really come through. Somewhere between the high ideals of the board and the operational practice of the guys on the ground there is something missing". You know I could have actually expanded a great deal more on it but I had annoyed them enough, they were very angry. Because of course they don't like to be told things, as you know with an audit committee, they like to be told that it was a problem but it is now sorted, so it isn't really a problem, so you can go home and sleep sound. (U)

The biggest weakness in corporate governance is the audit committee's lack of knowledge about what internal audit does. They get fooled by methodologies and spin and tend to think of things in black and white terms encouraged by salesmen from the Big Five. (R)

Relationships and engagement with other risk functions (Grid 10)

Although internal audit spoke of risk management as if it were an integrated business process, it frequently transpired that there were other risk functions within the business. In some instances internal audit worked closely with these regimes, sometimes not.

> *... audit have passed over responsibility for risk to our group risk manager, who is not in internal audit, so I find it an unusual situation. We have a division who are primarily concerned with minimising the amount of insurance that we have to pay ... for one reason or another the head of that division has now been given the title of group risk manager and he now has responsibility for ensuring that the company embeds risk management, because it was seen that it was a conflict of responsibilities if we did it, because we were auditing it. But I know a lot of internal audits have actually worked quite hard and helped to develop risk management policies and procedures ... and I think it is a shame because, you know, we are driving it, we are running the workshops, you know, we are doing the audit work, but we have somebody else now who is actually pushing processes through. And we will work with him, don't get me wrong, I mean, I wave to him as we are are walking down to the canteen, we are great friends and we do work together, but that is the way it has gone.* (M)

Health and safety functions tended to be relatively separate as did risk functions dealing with physical processes. Relationships with insurance functions were closer, although many of them reported to the company secretary or solicitor rather than to the financial director. In one company at least internal audit carried out audits of the processes used by the other risk functions, but this was not universal.

As previously mentioned Hood *et al.* (2001) have noted that risk regulation regimes adopt different styles and are frequently isolated from each other. Some risks are covered by legislation, such as health and safety, mandatory insurance (*eg* employers' liability) and there are specific rules for different industries and processes. External regulation seemed to be one factor which separated a particular risk function from others.

In some companies, internal audit covered the processes used by different risk processes as part of its functions. In other companies it was less clear how assurance about the operation of these processes was achieved. In some cases other risk functions reported to the audit committee, in others they reported to the board.

It is apparent that, with diverse reporting lines, an overall picture of risk cannot be achieved below the level of the board and it did not seem that many, if any, of the companies had achieved an integrated system of internal control and risk-management as apparently envisaged by the Turnbull report.

Involvement of internal audit in strategy (Grid 11)

Some interviewees felt the introduction of risk-management processes had had a positive impact on their company's strategic decision making; no longer was it down to the 'gut feel' of the chairman. However, the interviewees had little involvement in strategic processes. The interviewees were asked specifically about this area because it had been brought up by one of the initial interviewees (Company U) and because there had been indications that an effect of the introduction of business risk auditing had been to encourage external auditors to offer strategic advice. Some interviewees were clear that this was beyond the remit of internal audit, while others had a different view:

> *We don't do any work really at looking at the strategic build and direction of the company. Now my personal view of this is that we are missing a trick there, but it is a very, very difficult area to audit. We don't actually have a great deal of interaction … when the strategic plan is built, they are asked to identify the key risks in the strategy*

and we try to get the risk workshop timed so that when they are building the strategic plan they are performing a risk workshop so it actually feeds into the strategic plan build and also into the timing of the putting together of our audit plan, but it doesn't always work that way. That really is the only sort of interaction between the two, we don't audit the strategy. (M)

I think we are being pulled more in the direction of strategy. The improvements we suggest require to be incorporated in an execution matrix. We make a contribution to the implementation of strategy – we are a lot closer to strategy than compliance. What we do is identify the riskiness [inherent in strategy] and feed it into our processes. (G)

In another company, internal audit had reviewed board processes:

We are just finishing at the moment an audit of the risk that the board becomes ineffective, so inappropriate structures, inappropriate membership and internal conflict, and we have looked at the mechanisms that the board has, that they use to manage the risk internally. That's the most difficult one we have ever done, because we are not experts in that, in fact very few people are, but what we have done is to interview the directors, talked to them, get their ideas, consolidate them, just as you are doing with me now, and then we played it back to them, and we said "Well these are the things you have said are the key issues, and we have done a very short questionnaire, and what do you think about these", just, you know, five little questions on a note to all the directors and then they come back. Because as we serve them we can't actually audit them as they are our masters, but what we are doing is holding a mirror up to them saying "Look you can reflect or pass back to yourselves collectively in an anonymous way". (Q)

Involvement in strategy had implications for the independence of internal audit:

> ... it is not us who is making the decisions, the strategic decisions, so we may advise but we would not be a decision taker or maker, and our advice, as I said, is generally far more from the controls aspects point of view anyway, in terms of this is something we are looking at, what are the internal audit considerations regarding this, you know, to see which way we go on this decision. So no, I feel quite comfortable about our independence, more so now actually, since de-merger and since we are a group audit function reporting directly into the audit committee. (H)

> ... it's been a struggle because, again, you're working on a project and trying to remain independent of that project from an audit perspective, but also you do have definite interests in getting the controls going. (P)

Summary

In this chapter the analysis of the interview data has been presented in a format linked to the principal areas covered by the research questions. The use of a grounded theory approach as described in chapter three sensitised the emergence of a further range of issues which had not originally been identified as central to the study. These themes emerged during the analysis process and relate to fundamental aspects of internal audit work and its context which have not been widely addressed in either the academic or the professional literature. These are discussed in chapter six.

CHAPTER SIX

EMERGING ISSUES: EDUCATION, COMMUNICATION, INDEPENDENCE AND CHANGE

This chapter draws out further dimensions of internal audit which emerged from the second and third phases of research.

It is of the essence of qualitative research such as this that the outcome is not statistical generalisations but theoretical ones (Yin, 1994); the findings cannot be projected from a sample onto a wider population of companies but, through the research process, a refined theory is developed which provides a richer explanation and understanding of the phenomenon under investigation. The questions which formed the basis for the interviews (see Appendix One) provided an initial framework for analysis, but the iterations of the coding process and development of categories provided further insights which have been characterised as relating to the importance of education and development, communication and independence in the work of auditors, and the pervasive influence of endemic change in determining what auditors do and how they do it.

Education and development (Grid 12)

> *There is always an element of training in any auditor's portfolio ... (P)*

The educative category of activity arose in several guises. Educating line managers to ensure shared understanding was vital:

The problem we had was people didn't understand what a control was, and what they'd write in the management control column was a great sort of taradiddle about what they did every day. At nine o'clock I open the post and off it would go. Then, of course, they were complaining that it was getting too voluminous, so we had to work quite hard with them to explain to them the difference between an action and a control and what it was we were trying to get to. (A)

The heads have been trained and educated in looking at risk as a result of the initial training, initial workshops that we've all been through to get to that stage. (I)

The use of risk management software also led to a training requirement:

The idea of us going out there and visiting them and working through it with them, should, hopefully, enable them to start using the software and processes in a way that we had originally envisaged. (K)

An internally-based education role resulted from the process of drawing people into internal audit, either from within the business or as recruits to it, providing them with wide-ranging experience of the business and its systems and returning them to a line management role with a greater understanding of the business. This activity was viewed as a very important contribution to the organisation, a significant way in which internal audit provided added value.

They're going round seeing different aspects of a business and then hopefully we'd move them into a line role when they've got a good grounding of most areas of the business. (C)

The idea that [I] always had when I came to work here … was that you would spend perhaps 18 months or so in internal audit and then move into a different part of the business. Use that time: (a) to do the assurance role; and (b) to learn about lots of different parts of the business, and then hopefully you can be useful to the business in working in one of those other areas. I wouldn't want to do it for ever, I've been doing it for a year or so now, sometime after another six months, I'd be looking to do something slightly different in [K]. There's a number of people within this building who have done my job. (K)

I want the businesses to actually see a spell in business process review as a career development opportunity, if they have got a high potential. ... I see it as part of my role to develop up a talent pool for tomorrow's leaders for the organisation. (S)

In some companies a secondment to internal audit was viewed as an important step in developing "high-fliers" in the organisation:

So we try to get mainly from those core areas from inside the business, IT, marketing, production, to come into the internal audit group, not with just limited experience, but hopefully with a breadth of experience that they can bring to the audit function. So from a development standpoint, from a business, they are already kind of developed, all we do is to teach them how to practice the audit methodology ... the marketing people now realise ... the value that they gained by having someone come in to audit, because they are no longer marketing people, they are really good business people, they know the manufacturing side, they know the whole business really, they really understand the business a whole lot better than when they came in. So they are really willing to give us the top people. (T)

But this could also present problems:

The problem we had was because we wanted people at 30 years old, say, in their line job they were managers in charge of a team of people. Of course, they come into audit and they're the most junior people on the block, because they don't know what they're doing. And that's OK for six months while they're learning the ropes, they will accept that while they're still doing their training and everything.

But then, they want to be in charge of something, but they've still not really got good enough audit skills to necessarily be managers and, of course, you've only got so many managers slots and they're probably filled. So, it never worked out very satisfactorily. (A)

The process of bringing staff into an organisation and providing them with a role that enables them to work in and understand different parts of the organisation is a key process in 'indoctrinating' (Mintzberg, 2000) staff so that they assimilate the culture and values of the organisation. Other examples of the same process are some management trainee schemes and the training of young doctors through placement on a succession of different 'firms'. The process is particularly important where shared culture is key to achieving business objectives and staff work relatively independently or at remote locations.

Communication (Grids 13, 14, 15)

The communication role of the internal auditor is pervasive and multifaceted. It manifests itself both in the descriptions of what the auditor does and the language used by the interviewees. Two canonical activities of internal auditors are 'workshops' and 'presentations'.

Workshops are generally 'facilitated' by the auditors where people 'get issues out on the table'. The organisation and operation of workshops varied with the range and seniority level of participants:

Organising a workshop we start with the risk and the question, 'What is the control framework which mitigates such and such a risk?' This generates a control objective – eg data integrity. At that point we determine a workshop leader – somebody who has responsibility in the area – and create an invitation list for participants in the workshop. The invitation list is a cross-slice of people from different levels and functions concerned with the risk. We also ask along some (generally internal) suppliers and customers who relate to the area concerned. There are also some people from support areas asked along, for example IT or HR. The leader starts with an opening address asking people to be open and honest; the internal auditor facilitates. What follows includes brainstorming which gets out into the open what other people might call 'weaknesses', but which in our terms are 'issues'... People want to talk about the things that affect them. They want to tell you what their problems are. (G)

... when we run the risk workshops with the senior managers, we use a number of questions to get them thinking out of the box. Things like what would you hate to see reported in the press, what near misses have you or your competitors had in recent years, what are the legal issues in your job. ... we had a list of all the controls, all the areas of risks, and we used to hand it out at the workshop ... and that went down like a lead balloon so we don't do that any more, so we try and do it more subtly. (M)

Some participants were reluctant and needed to be convinced of the value of the workshop process:

Some people we had to drag kicking and screaming to a workshop, and when we had the Turnbull report it was easier for us to do that, because we had something that said to them, we need to do this because the company needs to be able to identify, evaluate and manage its risks. (M)

The first thing we said was we need your executive team to spend half a day. "What!!" but we persuaded a couple of them to have a go at it and they found it so helpful that word spread like wildfire and we were absolutely swamped with requests to go and facilitate workshops. (A)

Workshops are designed to be cross-functional and sometimes range across the entire organisation. The purposes of these workshops are to discover and describe risks not previously known, to (re-)valuate known risks and sometimes to arrive at tentative management alternatives.

> *So it has been trying to understand the dynamics of, if you like, the collective risk profile for the group, for example, we needed to gather information … how risky is the business, is there something else that is more likely to impact or whatever, so we needed to understand all of the differences and the similarities of what each business brings to the group's portfolio. (S)*

Workshops are also regarded as a powerful means of horizontal communication in business and form a basis for upward 'presentations', typically to the audit committee or to a risk committee or other gatherings of senior management.

> *… an example would be I did a presentation to one of the boards and we talked about that particular management's approach to risk and control and governance and all of that kind of stuff. (S)*

> *… the next milestone, if you like, is a risk workshop for the executive committee next week, which will take the results of the individual conversations with the individual executive members and present them with a group risk in a format which we hope they will buy into. (F)*

While acting as a communication channel within the organisation, assisting in the identification and classification of risk and the dissemination of a common understanding, internal auditors also communicate information brought in from outside the organisation through benchmarking internal control processes against those of other companies.

Other forms of communication include face to face meetings with senior management in operating divisions – often it appeared that such meetings were the major source of information for audit reports. The majority of such interchanges appeared to be co-operative, although auditors did speak of occasional wariness or reluctance to talk by operating unit managers. However, auditors saw their role as one of being there to help and that it was part of their job to convince managers of this. This view contrasts with the idea that it is the function of auditors to be stern, critical and disciplinarian in their approach, as a way of enforcing compliance with company policy. In keeping with this assistance role, the interviewees described much of their activity as "facilitation".

Facilitation extends to all levels of the organisation, including the board. As previously noted, one respondent said:

> *We are just finishing at the moment an audit of the risk that the board becomes ineffective, so inappropriate structures, inappropriate membership and internal conflict, and we have looked at the mechanisms that the board has, that they use to manage the risk internally ... as we serve them, we can't actually audit them as they are our masters, but what we are doing is holding a mirror up to them.* (Q)

Facilitation also takes place in the context of managing change, especially that following acquisitions or demergers. The distinction between facilitation and review roles requires "changing hats":

> *We had two distinct processes, two distinct teams, two distinct cultures, that type of thing that had to be brought together and integrated. So we have played, I think, clearly a supportive role to the management team, we have dropped into a lot of facilitation work with them. My firm belief is that we are here to support management meet the business objectives at a sensible efficiency and level of effectiveness; our philosophy is not to sort of come in and beat them up, we would rather be up front and facilitate rather than react ... we have challenged them on a lot of their change initiatives, looked at their process around, if you like, driving change, effectiveness of communication we have observed ... We have also put on a strict review hat as well, in that we*

have gone in and actually looked at specific areas of, particularly, the management framework, which we felt would complement the work that we were doing to give the Managing Director and his people a more comprehensive understanding of risk and control issues. (S)

Juggling with this contrast in roles is a challenge that internal audit faces in its continuing need to demonstrate added value. This is clearly recognised in the IIA Position Statement (Institute of Internal Auditors, 2002).

Primary responsibility for risk-management lies with line management. Internal audit's involvement should stop short of responsibility and accountability for risk-management across the organisation and of managing risks on management's behalf. However, in order to add value, it is often beneficial for internal audit to give proactive advice or to coach management on embedding risk management processes into business activities.

Independence (Grid 16)

The independence of internal audit is an important factor in its claim to professional status and can be characterised in various ways: operational independence from management processes, independence of reporting line and independence as an individual's state of mind. Attribute Standard 1100 of Professional Practice of Internal Auditing promulgated by the Institute of Internal Auditors (UK) requires that 'internal audit activity should be independent, and internal auditors should be objective in performing their work'.

As already shown, the internal auditors interviewed were usually not wholly independent from management processes. Typically they engaged in other activities, such as process review, which would lead them to audit processes that they themselves had recommended and perhaps designed. Internal auditors undertook 'consulting' activity or worked with departments to implement new systems. Internal auditors facilitated and took part in risk identification and assessment activities which were important parts of their businesses' management and control systems.

Internal auditors had mixed views about this. On the one hand some recognised that complete independence was not possible.

> *You can't be independent of a person who's paying you at the end of the day. But you have to be prepared to stand your ground, you know, even though it is your boss who's the finance director or the chief executive, or whoever it is you report to. If you believe that what you're trying to tell him is right and he's wrong, then you have to be prepared to stick with it and you have to be prepared to go to the chairman of the audit committee and say, the finance director and I are having a disagreement about this because, from an audit perspective, I think X and he thinks Y. (A)*

At least two companies fiercely guarded the independence of internal audit, indicated by reporting directly to the audit committee rather than *via* the finance function.

> *We are completely independent. ... We all work for the audit committee. (B)*

> *I feel quite comfortable now we are a group function reporting directly to the audit committee. (H)*

Some auditors had firm views about activities that would compromise their independence. For example, one interviewee distinguished strongly between internal audit and management:

> *Risk-management is part of management assurance and internal audit should be communicating totally with the risk-management function, but has to be independent ... it is management's role to ensure that the controls they are relying on to mitigate those risks are actually working and are effective.*

... and then my role is to provide independent assurance on the effectiveness of the management of all business risks. (Q)

And another said:

I don't want our guy writing policy and procedures. (P)

But at the same time a certain closeness to management was desirable and an excessive concentration on independence would mean that the auditors would:

... Get removed from the reality of the business. (N)

You have to get your hands dirty and actually get in there and add something to the process. (P)

This state of qualified independence seemed to demonstrate commitment to the organisation and was inherent in an advisory role. Even so, internal audit could be more independent than external audit and was not a 'vested interest'. (P)

External auditors can do consultancy – I don't see internal audit doing that. (G)

Change (Grids 17, 18, 19)

Change was a constant theme that emerged from the interviews. Few of the internal auditors had been in a stable environment for very long. Several of them had changed jobs in the recent past and in other cases there had been significant changes to the organisation in which they were working.

The principal changes that had impacted upon internal audit were changes to the group structure – most notably acquisitions and demergers - or to the organisation of internal audit itself. Nearly all of the organisations had been involved in significant acquisitions or demergers during the last three years. In the case of acquisitions there was a need to integrate the acquired company into the group and, despite due diligence, a need to find out exactly what had been acquired, the risks associated with the new company and its existing control processes.

We wouldn't be involved in the due diligence up front, but what they'd do is, as soon as they bought it, they'd put in what they called a 'SWAT' team, which was an auditor, a legal person, a production guy, a quality, … a selection of people, just to go in and in a week, do a quick and dirty round the place, and report back to management. (A)

In the case of demergers, there was a need to set up an internal audit function from scratch or, in one case, to outsource internal audit.

So it was relatively new, it was a new board, I'd only just then been appointed as head of internal audit for the group, as opposed to the UK. The risk committee obviously was new, everything was fairly new at that stage. (H)

In one case a significant part of the organisation had been demerged which had simplified internal audit of the remaining part of the organisation greatly and the internal audit function was adapting to that change.

Changes in organisational operations and structure, changes in board, audit committee and internal audit personnel and changes in corporate governance reporting requirements had all had an impact on the working environment of the interviewees. Where acquisitions or de-mergers had led to significant organisational change within the group, centralisation of internal audit often followed, with a new head of internal audit (or an equivalent function such as "process review"). In groups of companies, practice sometimes varied across the group, with some in-house and some outsourced internal audit and this needed to be standardised.

> *There had been different approaches to internal audit, so the Finance Director of the UK had taken the decision that he wanted an in-house function, others were going for peer review type internal audit work, more informal really. Some were actually outsourcing to our external auditors ... to come in and conduct internal audit review work. So there had been a bit of a mish-mash of different ways of addressing internal audit and it was very much left to each division as to the way they wanted to do it. (H)*

In several companies, the introduction of Turnbull reporting coincided conveniently with such an internal change process, allowing the necessary systems to be put in place alongside the commencement of a new operating procedure.

> *I guess there were a number of changes. One was in terms of reporting, in terms of changing the grading of the reports, the structure of the reports, prioritising recommendations. Secondly, in terms of the way that people did jobs, placing a lot greater importance on planning. People certainly, when they went overseas, used to do something which I call parachuting in, which is basically, I guess, go with their auditor's toolkit, parachute into a country and then decide what they wanted to do while they were on the ground. So I put a lot more priority in terms of planning and risk rating of individual areas of the businesses, so that we know we focus on the key risks within individual businesses, the important areas within individual businesses, and because one of the things that happened in the past was that they basically had a standard programme which they went in and what you found over a period of time is that certain people had certain interests in certain areas of the business and that's where we focused on. (J)*

Significant changes were taking place in the work of internal audit. In some cases, the internal audit function had taken an explicit role in the change management process:

... last March we acquired one of our key competitors in the UK ... it has been quite an exciting time and to me that's exactly where this function fits in because we should be, if you like, leading and facilitating and supporting management through change. Because the bottom line is that that's always the riskiest thing that you are faced with, so change and integration and so on. We had two distinct processes, two distinct teams, two distinct cultures, that type of thing that had to be brought together and integrated. So we have played, I think, clearly a supportive role to the management team, we have dropped into a lot of facilitation work with them ... You know, we have challenged them on a lot of their change initiatives, looked at their process around, if you like, driving change, effectiveness of communication we have observed. (S)

The role of compliance testing was often viewed as far less important:

I think there is still a reliance on internal audit to ... do quite traditional stock checking and float checking and stuff like that, and that is stuff where we don't add value and I don't want us to be really focusing on that. (H)

The traditional approach of tick and bash is that you do a lot of work to prove that control is in place, but probably don't come up with wonderfully commercial, productive output in your internal audit. You get this wonderful warm sense that you've got great controls in place, but they cost you the earth to get there and therefore are actually not worth doing. (I)

Responsibility for a lot of the work that people perceive as being internal audit work, in other words compliance, would be positioned totally with line management and they would choose from a range of techniques to monitor compliance. Not necessarily using "auditors" or "policemen". They could use self-assessment, peer reviews, information systems, whatever is most effective. (Q)

Although there was an alternative view:

I believe any internal audit function, no matter what else it may progress to, should never lose sight of the fact that from a management point of view, that is a very valuable assurance that you can give. They do want to know that the basic control structure is in place, and appropriate, and functioning. (B)

Interviewees also reported the need to reframe perceptions of internal audit within their organisations, accompanying the operational changes:

When I first came in people said "Why do you need to look at this and why do you need to look at that", and now we actually get people contacting us and saying "Could you put somebody onto this project, and could I get somebody to just cast their eye over this and, you know, give us internal audits perspective on it?", so I am actually at the point now when I have to say, no we can't. People always think that they know what internal audit is about, and generally it is nothing like what it is about, so I'm trying to dispel some of the myths ... [like] thinking that you are there to catch them out and trip them up. (H)

But I think sometimes we're seen as the brake, if you like. I think they see us as an obstacle to get over at times. (P)

Several of the interviewees distinguished "reviews" from audit. Reviews appeared to be focused on particular aspects of the business or operating units and were frequently *ad hoc* rather than pre-planned parts of the work programme. They seemed to be less evidence-based than audits. However, the term review might not have been interpreted in the same way in different organisations. Changes to internal audit departments were also associated with changes to personnel, either in the internal audit department itself or, for example, changes of chief executive officer or financial director.

Summary

This chapter has presented themes which emerged in the course of the research. In qualitative research these new ways of looking at the investigation often contain valuable insights and opportunities for developing existing theories. The next chapter summarises the findings and develops the theme of change as a prelude to describing new roles for internal audit that were found in the course of the research.

CHAPTER SEVEN

CONCLUSION

The analysis of interview data described in the previous chapters demonstrates the range and variety of structures and activities that characterise internal audit in the target companies. A rich picture has emerged of the ways in which internal audit is conducted, its involvement in the risk management process and its organisational relationships. This chapter highlights the important features of the internal audit landscape under the following headings:

- Turnbull and Turnbull disclosures

- Risk identification, assessment and management

- Organisation of internal audit and its current role

- The crystallisation of risks, relationships and engagement with boards and audit committees and other risk functions

- Involvement of internal audit in strategy

- Education and development

- Communication

- Independence

- Change

- New roles of internal audit

- Limitations of the research

Turnbull and Turnbull disclosures

Where companies had already embraced risk-based approaches to internal audit, internal auditors thought that their companies needed to undertake very little adjustment in order to become "Turnbull compliant". The systems needed to provide boards with assurance about the effectiveness of internal controls were already in place and merely needed to be formalised, perhaps through clarification of reporting lines, the reconfiguration of an existing risk committee or awareness-raising sessions, often facilitated by internal audit.

In other companies where risk management systems were at an earlier, embryonic stage, the impact was more significant, possibly requiring the establishment of a risk committee, closer co-ordination between differing areas where risk had traditionally been dealt with and more intensive training. The impact on some, usually smaller, companies seemed to have been greater in terms of changes in process and there were indications of increased costs.

Internal auditors generally viewed Turnbull as beneficial to their cause and said it had helped to alter the perceptions of internal audit in a positive way, so that operating departments frequently sought the advice of internal audit when implementing new or changed processes. Turnbull did not, however, appear to have provided the platform for major developments in the authority and standing of internal audit that might have been expected, given the exhortatory tone of the professional literature noted in chapter one. Commentators are now suggesting that the Smith Report on audit committees will provide a further boost: a survey conducted in May 2003 reported that many heads of internal audit believed that Smith would increase the status of internal audit as well as audit committees (Piper, 2003).

The Turnbull treatment of internal control and risk-management as effectively synonymous seems to be a reflection of existing practice within the companies included in this study, rather than an indication of a sudden change in perspective as might be concluded from a study of UK corporate governance policy documents from the Cadbury Report onwards.

Risk identification, assessment and management

In the companies studied, risk management procedures were at varying stages of development. The risk identification and assessment process generally included the production of risk registers in various guises, either maintained centrally or at operating units. Risk assessment was usually based on expected value of impact principles but the assessment was frequently summarised in the form of a score, a matrix, or 'traffic lights'.

The relationship of internal audit with the risk-management process varied from that of outside observer to influential insider. However, movement towards the integration of internal audit with risk-management was clearly identified in the testing of the model of the relationship between company and internal audit approaches to risk-management. Internal auditors were asked how they rated their approach to work on a scale ranging between highly compliance-based to highly risk-based, and how they rated their company's approach to risk on a scale ranging from reactive to holistic. Most interviewees placed both themselves and their companies at or above the mid-point of the scales, but nearly all felt that they and their companies were moving up the scales and that this movement towards risk-based management and auditing was desirable.

Internal auditors had important roles as facilitators and organisers of risk identification and assessment, generally through workshops. When adverse events occurred ('crystallisation of risk') internal audit was frequently involved in reporting on events and making recommendations for improved controls.

Those organisations which made risk management a responsibility of line managers seemed to use it as a key tool. Consciousness of risks and reporting on risks as well as profits were integral to the management of some of the organisations. In these organisations, however, internal audit tended to be 'out of the loop'; it audited risk-management but was not itself part of the process.

Risk management appears to be a rational response to change. Pushing responsibility for risk down the organisation makes for quicker response and possibly some portfolio diversification – if managers have diverse responses to risk, it is less likely that they will all be wrong. From a cybernetic perspective, speed of response is important since (informally stated) negative feedback can only maintain stability if the speed of response is more than twice as fast as the pace of change.

As Hood *et al.* (2001) have pointed out, risk regulation regimes are rarely integrated. This was true of risk management in the sample of companies. There were usually different risk management functions covering risks like 'health and safety', 'security', 'financial' and 'insurance'. Oversight of such risks generally came together only at board level and few organisations could truly be said to have integrated systems of internal control and risk management. Since the methodologies for assessing and controlling diverse risks are often very different, perhaps this is inevitable. The lack of a common means of assessing risk management calls into question whether company boards can be expected to offer meaningful opinions about whether their systems of risk management are effective.

It is evident that, within organisations, there are different understandings of terms such as 'risk management', 'assessment' and 'review' and that these understandings depend heavily on local circumstances. In this respect, the disclosures about companies' risk management procedures are difficult to interpret without considerable knowledge of the company and its management processes. Diversity of interpretation also suggests that there is much development of risk-management to be undertaken until it can be regarded as a process for which there is a commonly shared understanding among practitioners at large; risk management cannot be codified at present. One consequence of the diversity of practice and interpretation is that it has not been possible to form any 'general theory' of internal auditing or risk-management; given information about a company's lines of business and organisational structure, there does not seem to be a way of predicting what kind of risk management process it will adopt.

A further feature of the processes for risk identification and assessment is the way in which risks are filtered. Because it is necessary to summarise and consolidate risks for the purposes of upward reporting, risks of low probability, although possibly of high impact, may not be reported. Such risks are numerous and, taken together, the probability that one or more will occur is substantial, even if the individual probabilities are small. It follows that, despite having formalised risk management procedures, there remains a substantial risk, in most organisations, that a risk that has not been formally recognised will crystallise (a blind-side risk). Awareness of this may be a further reason why management and external auditors are unwilling to offer opinions about the effectiveness of systems.

Organisation of internal audit and its current role

Some companies had dedicated internal audit functions but the function was often combined with 'risk management', 'process review' or similar activities. Some auditors acknowledged a traditional compliance checking role but there was a widespread view that monitoring of compliance was a function that should, as far as possible, be the responsibility of line management.

Outsourcing of the entire internal audit function was rare in the companies examined, although 'co-sourcing' arrangements, in which external providers (generally audit firms) supplied expertise in specific areas such as IT, were fairly common. Surprisingly, the outsourcing arrangements encountered had been instigated by the internal audit function. None of the interviewees viewed the prospect of outsourcing as a threat, although in most companies the possible advantages were regularly reviewed. The view was generally expressed that providers of outsourced services neither understood the businesses they were auditing very well nor were they committed to it in the same way as in-house staff. Outsourcing of internal audit also meant forgoing most of the important educational and development benefits of internal audit.

The work programme of internal audit was, to a greater or lesser extent, an outcome of companies' risk identification and assessment processes in many of the companies. However, other factors, such as rotation of coverage and the priorities of the board or audit committee, also affected the design of the programme.

The crystallisation of risks, relationships and engagement with boards and audit committees and other risk functions

Some boards and audit committees were more proactive than others. All the internal audit reports were made available to audit committees and all heads of internal audit attended audit committee meetings.

Most companies had other risk functions apart from internal audit, such as health and safety and insurance. Where separate processes existed, integration of risk management could only occur at the level where the lines of reporting intersected, usually at board level. It did not appear that companies had achieved integrated systems of internal control and risk management as envisaged by the Turnbull Report.

Involvement of internal audit in strategy

In view of the role which external auditors seemed to be seeking as business advisers, the interviewees were asked about the level of involvement of internal audit in the formation and implementation of business strategy. Internal auditors did not have, nor did they seek, a prominent role in strategic decision making, although those who were more involved with process improvement thought that they had a role in implementation.

Education and development

Internal auditors saw three important educational roles: they trained their own staff, they educated line managers in control and risk management, and they provided a function where new entrants to the organisation, or existing staff, could spend a short period as a means of understanding the business. Although this feature of internal audit is well-known, the interviewees placed considerable emphasis on it.

Communication

Much of the activity which internal auditors undertook could be classified as communication, especially talking with divisional and business managers, running workshops and making presentations to senior management. The workshop, in particular, seemed to be an important way in which auditors facilitated the identification and assessment of risks or dealt with other issues.

Independence

Although a few of the interviewees fiercely guarded the independence of internal audit, refusing to accept ownership of processes or to undertake work which they felt would compromise their independence, most departments were involved in risk-management and process improvement in ways which meant that they would at some point be auditing processes where they had had a hand in the design or implementation. This qualified independence was viewed as beneficial although auditors were conscious of the need to maintain a balance. The direct line of reporting to the audit committee was seen as reinforcing independence and some auditors believed that they were more independent than the external auditors, who were often compromised by their business advisory role and their vested interest in selling additional services.

Change

Change is a key theme of the modern management literature, yet very little writing about it deals with the problem of controlling the organisation during that change process.

Derived from this literature there are a number of alternative stories that could be told. One story looks to change in the management styles of organisations from traditional bureaucracies to 'modern organisations' that have been characterised by various writers as, for example, learning organisations (Argyris, 1992). Such organisations are characterised by double and triple-loop learning, empowerment of the lower levels of the hierarchy and control through maintenance of corporate culture. In particular, in learning organisations, control is not a requirement to adhere to centrally set policies, but is exercised through a less explicit constraint on the activities of subsidiaries, designed to limit the possibility that they will endanger shareholder value. In such organisations, internal audit can have a role in providing the different kind of assurance needed.

Another story is that organisations are influenced by changing cultures and the management philosophies of the people at the top. In such a 'power-perspective' (Burnes, 2000) management retains control through defining what counts as knowledge in the organisation (for example, in the way the cost system defines surpluses and deficits) and by manipulation of the culture. Examples of dominant management philosophies are: 'shareholder value', 'activity based management', 'core competence', 'business process re-engineering' and so on. Such philosophies are apt to change with time either in response to external forces, changes in personnel or through mere fashion.

A third kind of story is that change in companies is driven by external events. Porter's five forces model of competitive strategy is one such story in which relative success or failure is driven by threat of new entrants to the business, influences of suppliers and customers, the existence or arrival of substitute products and the competitiveness of the industry (Porter, 1979).

It would be possible to interpret the data in the light of any of these stories. However, the internal auditors interviewed rarely referred to a dominant management philosophy or overt organisational culture. There was no evidence that the organisations were changing in response to managerial perceptions of how organisations should be managed, except in two respects: (i) risk management was itself a key management approach in several of the organisations:

> *The chief executive, together with his direct reports, drive what we call the corporate risk profile* (S);

and (ii) one organisation was driven by 'shareholder value".

The above is not to say that strategic business choices of management are not important: acquisitions and demergers, for example, are clearly strategic choices. In one case there was a clear choice to focus on particular businesses and a wish to dispose of the parts of the group which did not fit; in two cases, however, demergers were effectively forced on the businesses because of past strategic errors and, in a further case where businesses were being disposed of because of a failure to control an important project (ironically, this had led to a reduction in the size of the internal audit department as a cost saving measure).

The endemic nature of change is clearly important for the interpretation of the roles of internal audit. One interpretation is that the traditional role of internal audit has gradually fallen away, in many companies, not because it has been replaced by something better but because it has become too difficult. It has become difficult because of the increase in the pace of change in organisations and technological change. In this scenario, internal audit may move furthest from the traditional role in organisations that had suffered considerable change and that employed the most sophisticated computerised transaction processing.

Another (not exclusive) interpretation is that internal audit has adapted in a functionally supportive role to enable organisations to cope, and possibly take advantage of, their increasingly dynamic environment.

New roles of internal audit

The diversity of these findings means that, although the Turnbull Report has significantly raised the profile of internal audit in organisations by highlighting its role in internal control and risk management, the organisational role of internal audit varies widely. The role of stern enforcer of compliance with company systems has largely been abandoned, wherever it existed, but has not been replaced by a uniform model.

Internal audit provides some useful organisational tools for management in a dynamic environment.

The role of internal audit

Internal auditors are uniquely placed to discover and evaluate the systems used in different parts of the organisation and to recommend adoption of the best of them in other parts of the organisation. This may be quicker and cheaper than developing systems centrally in many cases. In summary:

- The Turnbull requirements have led to an increased focus on internal audit and risk management.

- The traditional training role of internal audit continues to be important.

- Internal audit has a strong relationship with the audit committee, often with direct reporting channels.

- Internal auditors see their role as providing comfort and assurance on controls and a facilitation service, rather than reducing fraud and enforcing compliance.

- Although internal auditors increasingly review board processes, their work does not extend to evaluating strategic decisions.

- Because internal audit is used as a training ground, often for high fliers, staff turnover is relatively rapid.

- Outsourcing is seen as an economical solution for smaller companies. However, internal auditors sometimes consider that providers of outsourced internal audit do not understand the business and are not fully committed to the organisation. Their independence is also an issue if they are providing assurance or other services.

Internal audit and risk management

Both through normal patterns of work and through specific exercises such as workshops, internal auditors can identify the risks that are not necessarily caught through other formal processes or top-down reviews.

Some element of risk-based auditing is now almost universal in internal audit work and most auditors are also involved in companies' risk assessment. The Turnbull report has helped many companies to formalise these processes as follows:

- Internal auditors increasingly use risk-based frameworks to assess priorities and plan work.

- Internal auditors often aspire to integrate internal audit with risk management.

- Risk-based processes are particularly appropriate in dynamic situations where static design and implementation is impracticable.

- Management of risk varies across organisations. Internal audit is either part of the process or closely involved.

- A key role of internal audit is to facilitate workshops that are cross-functional and are used to discover or evaluate risks.

- Workshops are important for risk discovery and assessment and feed into risk management.

- Models of "expected-value frameworks" are produced that evaluate the impact and probability of occurrence.

- Often the risks identified are combined and edited for the Board to review. This results in a tendency for the numerous high impact/low probability risks to be ignored by the Board.

- The crystallisation of risks is often used as a learning experience.

- Some categories of risk, particularly those subject to external regulation, such as health and safety and insurance, are often treated separately from others.

- An integrated system of internal control and risk management is lacking in most organisations.

Internal audit and organisational change

As mentioned above, many organisations seek to give more responsibility to operating units and rely more on the strength of the organisational culture to maintain control than was previously the case. Internal audit, by visiting different units, by communicating widely and by training future managers can help to instil an organisation-wide culture. In particular:

- Champions of change often make use of internal audit.

- Internal audit has a key role in assisting the organisation to cope with a rapidly changing environment.

All of the above demonstrate that the role of internal audit has become increasingly important following the corporate governance reforms of the 1990s and it is likely that the role of internal audit will become more important in the future.

Limitations of the research

While this overall picture dovetails with the representation of change in internal audit in the commentaries and professional literature cited earlier, it should be recognised that the scope of the study is limited to exploring the perceptions of internal auditors and those responsible for the internal audit function in large commercial organisations: incorporation of the views of finance directors, audit committee members and internal audit clients, together with work in government and not-for-profit organisations, would present a more rounded picture and should be subject to further research.

REFERENCES

Adams, J (1995), *Risk*, UCL Press, London.

Argyris, C (1992), *On organizational learning*, Blackwell, Oxford.

Beck, U (1998), *The Politics of Risk Society*, in J Franklin (Ed.), *The Politics of Risk Society*, Polity Press, London.

Blackburn, S (1999), *Managing risk and achieving Turnbull compliance*, ABG, London.

Bou-Raad, G (2000), "Internal auditors and a value-added approach: the new business regime", *Managerial Auditing Journal,* 15(4).

Bruce, R (1998), "Hampel offers up a big serving of fudge", *The Times,* 5 February, p.30.

Burnes, B (2000), *Managing Change: a Strategic Approach to Organisational Dynamics* (3rd ed.), Pearson Education, Edinburgh.

Cadbury Committee (1992), *Report of the Committee on the Financial Aspects of Corporate Governance*, Gee, London.

Canadian Institute of Chartered Accountants, (1999), *Guidance on Control*, CICA, Toronto.

Chambers, A (1997), "Directors' reports on internal financial control", in *Financial Reporting 1995/96*, ICAEW, London.

Chambers, A D (2000), "Internal audit and risk management: impact on internal audit - development or revolution?", *Internal Control,* 32, pp.3-7.

COSO (2004), *Enterprise Risk Management Framework* Exposure Draft, retrieved 20 April 2004 from http://www.erm.coso.org/Coso/coserm.nsf/frmWebCOSOExecSum?ReadForm.

Deloitte and Touche Tohmatsu (2000), *Achieving Internal Audit Excellence*, Deloitte and Touche Tohmatsu, Wellington, NZ.

Douglas, M (1986), *Risk Acceptability According to the Social Sciences*, Routledge, London.

Douglas, M (1992), *Risk and Blame: Essays in Cultural Theory*, Routledge, London.

Douglas, M (1999), *Implicit Meanings*, Routledge, London.

Fogarty, T J & L P Kalbers, (2000), "An empirical evaluation of the interpersonal and organisational correlates of professionalism in internal auditing", *Accounting and Business Research,* 30(2), pp.125–136.

Griffiths, P (1999), "Understanding the expectations of finance directors towards internal audit and its future", *Managerial Auditing Journal,* 14(9), pp.489–496.

Hampel Committee (1998), *Committee on Corporate Governance, Final Report*, Gee, London.

Hermanson, H M (2000), "An Analysis of the Demand for Reporting on Internal Control", *Accounting Horizons,* 14(3), pp.325–341.

Hood, C, H Rothstein & R Baldwin (2001), *The Government of Risk*, Oxford University Press, Oxford.

ICAS (1993), *Auditing into the twenty-first century,* (ed W M McInnes), A Discussion Document of the Research Committee of the Institute of Chartered Accountants of Scotland, ICAS, Edinburgh.

ICAEW (2000), *Risk Management and the value added by Internal Audit*, ICAEW, London.

ICAEW Steering Group on the Financial Reporting of Risk (1999), *No Surprises,* ICAEW, London.

ICAEW (1997), *Financial reporting of risk- proposals for a statement of business risk*, Financial Reporting Committee Steering Group, ICAEW, London.

Institute of Internal Auditors (2002), *Position Statement on the Role of Internal Audit in Risk Management*, from http://www.iia.org.uk.

Jones, M & G Sutherland (1999), *Implementing Turnbull: A Boardroom Briefing*, ICAEW, London.

Kalbers, L P & T J Fogarty (1995), "Professionalism and its consequences: a study of internal auditors", *Auditing,* 14(1), pp.64–86.

KPMG (1999), *Transforming internal audit from its compliance role into a strategic organizational tool*, KPMG, London.

Lemon, W M, K W Tatum & W S Turley (2000), *Developments in the Audit Methodologies of Large Accounting Firms*, Auditing Practices Board, London.

Lilley, M & O Saleh (1999), "Making risk a rewarding business", *Internal Auditing*, (January), pp.18-20.

Maijoor, S (2000), "The Internal Control Explosion", *International Journal of Auditing*, 4, pp.101-109.

McNamee, D & T McNamee (1995), "The transformation of internal auditing", *Managerial Auditing Journal*, 10(2), pp.34-37.

Mintzberg, H (2000), *The Rise and Fall of Strategic Planning*, Pearson Education, London.

Morgan, G (1979), "Internal Audit Role Conflict: A Pluralist View", *Managerial Finance*, 5(2), pp.160-170.

Parker, L D & B H Roffey, (1997), "Back to the drawing board: revisiting grounded theory and the everyday accountant's and manager's reality", *Accounting, Auditing and Accountability Journal*, 10(2), pp.212-247.

Pentland, B (2000), "Will auditors take over the world? Program, technique and the verification of everything", *Accounting, Organizations and Society*, 25, pp.307-312.

Piper, A (2003), "Room at the Top", *Internal Auditing and Business Risk* (July), pp.15-17.

Porter, M E (1979), "How competitive forces shape strategy", *Harvard Business Review*, 57(2), pp.137-145.

Power, M (1997), *The Audit Society*, Oxford University Press, Oxford.

Power, M (1999a), *The Audit Implosion: Regulating Risk from the Inside*, ICAEW, London.

PricewaterhouseCoopers (2003), *The Sarbanes-Oxley Act of 2002: strategies for meeting new internal control reporting challenges: a white paper*, PricewaterhouseCoopers, London.

Royal Society (1992), *Risk: Analysis, Perception and Management*, Royal Society, London.

Rutteman Committee (1994), *Internal Control and Financial Reporting: Guidance for Directors of Listed Companies Registered in the UK*, ICAEW, London.

Selim, G & D McNamee (1999), "The Risk Management and Internal Auditing Relationship: Developing and Validating a Model", *International Journal of Auditing*, 3, pp.159-174.

Short, H, K Keasey, M Wright & A Hull (1999), "Corporate governance: from accountability to enterprise", *Accounting and Business Research*, 29(4), pp.337-352.

Smallman, C (1996), "Risk and organizational behaviour: a research model", *Disaster Prevention and Management*, 5(2).

Spira, L F & M Page (2003), "Risk management: the reinvention of internal control and the changing role of internal audit", *Accounting, Auditing and Accountability Journal*, 16(4), pp.640-661.

Turnbull Committee (1999), *Internal control: Guidance for Directors on the Combined Code*, ICAEW, London.

Yin, R K (1994), *Case study research: design and methods* (2nd ed.), Sage, Thousand Oaks.

APPENDIX ONE

1. Preliminary information requested from interviewees.

The Turnbull Report, Internal Control and Risk Management: the Developing Role of Internal Audit

The topics we would like to discuss with you include:

How has IA developed in your business over the last 5-10 years?

Issues facing the internal audit profession generally, including risk management and the impact of the Turnbull reporting requirements.

Background data: we would be grateful if you would supply the following information:

Your name...

Your qualifications...

Your company..

Your job title...

How long have you held this post? ....

How many non-executive directors serve on your company's board?
....

Does the board have:

a)   an audit committee? .... If so, when was it established? ....

b)   a remuneration committee? .... If so, when was it established? ...

c)   a risk committee? ...... If so, when was it established?.............

To whom does the internal audit function report? ....

2. Interview questions

Is the internal audit function outsourced?

If yes, to whom?

Date outsourcing commenced

If IA is not outsourced:

What is the disciplinary composition of the IA team? (spread of qualifications and experience)

How is the IA programme of work negotiated?

Reasons for outsourcing or not outsourcing IA

Main issues dealt with in last year

What are your current risk management processes? What methodology is used?

How are risks classified? Who is involved in the identification and assessment of risk?

What happens when an adverse event/disaster happens ie. a risk materialises?

How does this affect the risk management process?

What is the relationship between risk management and risk assessment?

How is the effectiveness of the risk management process assessed?

What is the board's role in risk management?

What is the role of the audit committee in risk management?

Have there been any recent changes? If so, what drove such changes and how have they affected the role/position of internal audit and the audit committee?

What is the role of internal control systems in relation to risk?

Did complying with Turnbull require any changes in the way the company reported on internal control?

What is the role of internal audit in the company's processes for forming, revising and implementing the strategy of the business?

To what extent do the company's risk management processes contribute to its strategic strength and competitive advantage?

How did the company determine the form of its disclosure under Turnbull?

Who has taken the lead in formulating the company's Internal Control disclosures in the financial statements?

APPENDIX TWO

SELECTIVE CODING OF INTERNAL AUDIT AND RISK MANAGEMENT INTERVIEWS

These grids were constructed as the final part of the process of analysis of the transcripts and notes of the interviews. Each grid is in three columns. The first column contains selective codings of the concepts that were expressed in the interviews. Some of these concepts summarise thoughts which were expressed by several interviewees, others reflect the flavour of only one set of comments. The rows of the grids group concepts into categories and the final column contains the dimensions of variation within the categories. The dimensions are either expressed as end points of a continuum (*eg* 'IA centralised *vs* IA decentralised') or as variables which can vary from zero upwards (*eg* 'Speed of response', 'extent of use of risk based methods', 'extent of horizontal communication'). Sometimes a single expression is used to express more than one dimension (*eg* 'Seniority and diversity'). Each of the grids is headed with an overall category descriptor (see chapter 3 for further details).

1. Turnbull
2. Turnbull Disclosures
3. Risk Identification Assessment and Management
4. Internal Audit
5. Outsourcing
6. Internal Audit Teams
7. Negotiation of Audit Plan
8. Crystallisation
9. Relationships and engagement with Board and AC
10. Relationship with other risk functions

11. Strategy

12. Education and development (E&D)

13. Relationship with Auditees

14. Communication

15. Workshops

16. Independence

17. Compliance and review

18. Acquisitions and demergers

19. Change

Grid 1 Turnbull		
Concepts	**Categories**	**Dimensions and Properties**
Shook us and the bigwigs up Were already compliant Formalising processes	Impact of Turnbull	Large impact *vs* small impact
Encouragement of risk management	Contributions	
Formalisation of processes		Formalisation of existing processes
Assurance the only added bit		
Risk management strategy group/risk management committee set up as result		Strengthening risk management
Strengthening non-financial risk management		
Made CRSA easier		Communication with divisions
Communication with divisional heads/Used by divisions		
Helped change perceptions of IA		
Only a compliance thing Developing business is higher priority		

Grid 1 Turnbull		
Concepts	**Categories**	**Dimensions and Properties**
Problem for small companies – cost Necessary evil for small plcs	Cost of compliance	Cost of compliance with Turnbull
Use of external risk consultants (insurers) Help from EAs EAs contribution was zero.	Involvement of outsiders	Extent of external assistance

Grid 2 Turnbull Disclosures		
Concepts	**Categories**	**Dimensions and Properties**
Internal audit Financial Director Company Secretary External Auditors	Author of disclosures	Written by IA *vs* written in consultation *vs* no IA involvement
Honest with the shareholders Full disclosure Listed all the risks, but because of US listing Increasing interest from investors in risk mgt more of a driver Pressure for environmental disclosures	Extent of disclosure	Full disclosure *vs* minimal disclosure Turnbull determines disclosure *vs* other forces driving disclosure
Compliance with Turnbull Always the get out – no need to express an opinion	Compliance with Turnbull Board opinion on effectiveness of internal control and risk management	Compliant *vs* non-compliant (all complied) Opinion expressed *vs* no opinion expressed (none expressed an opinion)

Grid 3 Risk Identification Assessment and Management		
Concepts	**Categories**	**Dimensions and Properties**
Long established Recent	History of process	Well before Turnbull *vs* post-Turnbull
Value Chain Inventory of risk model Workshops SWOT analysis Divisions responsible for own risks CRSA Risk registers Risk universe Proprietary software	Risk Identification Methods	Systematic methods *vs* non-systematic Top down *vs* bottom-up
Workshops Risk Committee Divisional management Top management CRSA	Process for Risk Assessment	Within line management *vs* outside line management
Traffic Lights Matrix Score Risk Footprint Judgement Narrative statement	Risk Measurement and Prioritisation	Expected value based *vs* judgement based
Internal audit responsibility Company Secretary's responsibility Divisional responsibility AC keen to track risk scores over time	Ownership of risk identification and assessment	Internal audit key to process *vs* internal audit peripheral
Quarterly Six monthly Annually	Frequency of risk re-assessment	Frequency of reassessment

Grid 3 Risk Identification Assessment and Management		
Concepts	**Categories**	**Dimensions and Properties**
Risk management needs smartening Process needs reinvigorating Risk management process not prioritised by divisional management Not embedded Tendency for mgt to put risk on back burner	Embedding of risk management	Embedded *vs* not embedded
Hierarchy of controls Insurance Pre-contract risk assessment	Kinds of risk management	4Ts: Treat, Terminate, Tolerate or Transfer
Operating risks Health and safety Disaster risks Regulatory risk Country risk Quality of output Murkiness of corporate governance structure Treasury and currency risk Succession risk Pure risk Insurable risk Speculative (upside) risk Physical risks Security risks Brand risks Business risk	Kinds of risk	Pure risk *vs* speculative risk

Grid 4 Internal Audit		
Concepts	**Categories**	**Dimensions and Properties**
Internal audit performed by finance people for part of the time IA combined with process review IA combined with risk management 'Inside or outside risk management' Separate internal audit departments in different divisions	Organisation of IA	IA as separate function *vs* combined with other functions IA centralised *vs* IA decentralised
Reports *via* head of risk management to FD Reports to AC Reports to FD +/- 'dotted line' to AC	Reporting	Reporting towards Financial Director *vs* reporting to AC
Focusing on risk management All about risk and control Auditing processes Auditing controls Auditing compliance	Audit focus	Risk focus *vs* process focus *vs* compliance focus
Providing comfort Providing assurance Providing recommendations	Output	Assurance and accountability *vs* Process review

Grid 5 Outsourcing		
Concepts	**Categories**	**Dimensions and Properties**
Fully outsourced (O/s) Co-sourcing Internal audit manager only	Extent of outsourcing	All work done by IA *vs* all work done by O/s
Outsourcing not cost efficient for a large company Company too small to have a dedicated IA function O/s pressure to sell additional services	Cost efficiency	IA more cost efficient *vs* O/s more cost efficient
Specialised knowledge of business required O/s need to continually relearn the business IA know and belong to the business	Business specific knowledge	Internal knowledge and experience *vs* external knowledge and experience
IA have future career in house IA a career stepping stone	Commitment to business	High level of commitment to business among audit staff *vs* low level of commitment to business
Need for IS audit Availability of expertise as needed	Need for specialist knowledge/ expertise	High need for expertise *vs* low need for expertise
Not enough actionable recommendations Spreading best practice	Usefulness of recommendations	Useful recommendations *vs* recommendations of little use
O/s too financial accounting oriented O/s inflexible O/s always look at it as an external auditor	O/s biased towards external audit/ financial reporting	Business orientation *vs* financial reporting orientation

Grid 6 **Composition of Internal Audit Teams**		
Concepts	**Categories**	**Dimensions and Properties**
Tenure of manager Turnover of IA staff	Rate of staff turnover	Rapid turnover *vs* long tenure
Size of team	Size of team	Number of staff (varies from 1 to 85, most companies had from 4 to 7 IA staff)
Accountants IT/IS auditors H&S auditors Engineers Compliance officers Business analysts Risk managers	Disciplinary make up of IA team	All auditors accountants *vs* diverse backgrounds

Grid 7 **Negotiation of Audit Plan**		
Concepts	**Categories**	**Dimensions and Properties**
Falls out of risk matrix Covers specific risks Auditing most risky businesses Rate riskiness of businesses Three year rolling programme Not risk based	Basis of plan	Result of risk assessment process *vs* rotation-based Business-based *vs* function -based
Risk management falls out of audit plan Risk matrix follows internal audit visits	Contribution to risk management	Audit planning process contributes to risk management *vs* little contribution
Agreed with the AC AC doesn't question the plan much	Influence of audit committee (AC)	

Grid 8 Crystallisation of risks		
Concepts	**Categories**	**Dimensions and Properties**
Spot it coming Business has tried and tested processes Contingency plans Emergency response	Preparing for adverse events	Well prepared *eg* insured, contingency plans in place *vs* events not forecast and no preparation
Stop deterioration Resulting in review of risk management	Reacting to adverse events	Prompt and effective action to mitigate effects *vs* ineffective reaction
Investigation by IA (No) blame Follow up after a few months	Learning from adverse events	Blaming *vs* not blaming Extent of investigation of causes

Grid 9 Relationships and engagement with Boards and Audit Committees		
Concepts	**Categories**	**Dimensions and Properties**
With AC With Board Similarity of AC and Board Risk orientation of sponsor Requests for reviews Forcefulness of chair Political behaviour Information flow Frequency of meetings with, presentations and reports to sponsor	Other party proactive Other party seeking comfort Support for risk management	Active *vs* passive Impact on risk approach Directions of information flow

Grid 10 Relationship and engagement with other risk functions		
Concepts	Categories	Dimensions and Properties
Health and safety Environment Insurance Treasury Risk management Engineering production	Other functions	Number of other risk functions
Function done in line of management IA audits other risk functions IA doesn't dabble in treasury IA take an overall view of compliance with Turnbull	Relationship with other risk functions Reporting by other risk functions *eg* to AC or not Who audits whom?	Closeness and integration of risk functions

Grid 11 Involvement of internal audit in strategy		
Concepts	**Categories**	**Dimensions and Properties**
Risk management provides a clarity about risk Previously strategy formed by 'gut instinct' of chairman Risk workshops timed to coincide with strategic plan building	Impact of risk management on strategy	Changes strategic thinking *vs* no impact
Level below strategy – implementation Closer to strategy than compliance Little influence The Board is sovereign on risk It's a brave auditor who goes to the board and questions strategy Can't challenge CEO but can audit strategy forming process	Impact of IA on strategy	Significant impact *vs* little impact (no one claimed a significant impact)

Grid 12 Education and development (E&D)		
Concepts	**Categories**	**Dimensions and Properties**
E&D in risk management E&D in control and business processes	Training line managers in risk management and control	Significant role *vs* not important
Training IA, helping them to grow	Training IA staff	Significant role *vs* not important
Financially (not commercially) oriented people can come in and be some use Add some value while learning about commercial realities A typical route for new financial managers IA staff not moving on – too nice a job	Inducting and indoctrinating potential new managers	An important function *vs* few IA staff moving into line or financial management

Grid 13 Relationship with Auditees		
Concepts	**Categories**	**Dimensions and Properties**
Helping Coaching Training in risk	Assisting and educating	Outward communication
Selling risk management Persuading of value of advice Relations less negative IA welcomed and advice sought Non-threatening	Persuading and building confidence	Confidence building
Listening Understanding commercial imperative	Listening	Inward communication

Grid 14 Communication		
Concepts	**Categories**	**Dimensions and Properties**
Facilitating 'Getting issues out on the table' A main method of working	Workshops (see Grid xx)	Horizontal communication
Presentations to senior management/AC/risk committee	Presentations	
Talking to senior people Negotiating audit plan with general managers Challenging management	Talking to managers	Vertical communication
Audit reports Reviews Spreading best practice	Reporting	Creating shared perceptions and values

Grid 15 Workshops		
Concepts	Categories	Dimensions and Properties
Not boring management process Discovery of control framework Risk identification Aid board in signing off that risks reviewed	Risk management tool	Contribution to risk management
Senior level Multi-level Cross functional Involving outsiders *eg* customers and suppliers	Composition	Diversity and seniority
IA facilitates Participant facilitates Risk management function facilitates	Facilitation	Facilitated by IA *vs* not
Quantity of issues Importance of issues	Issues/risks arising	Number of issues/ risks identified and prioritised

Grid 16 Independence		
Concepts	**Categories**	**Dimensions and Properties**
Proportion of time on consulting projects Need for terms of reference on engagements IA more independent than external auditors Independence needed so external auditors can rely on IA	Independence from process change and implementation	Wholly independent *vs* consulting role *vs* participant role
IA not a vested interest (EA is) IA not writing policy and procedures Getting your hands dirty Involvement in process review Can have too much independence; IA can get removed from reality Can't be independent of paymasters Can be consultants and help business manage its control, but not own process More comfortable reporting to AC		
Should not own risk management Can facilitate, run workshops but should not make the judgement	Independence from risk management	

Grid 17 Change		
Concepts	**Categories**	**Dimensions and Properties**
Major acquisitions Major disposals Demerger of group Changes of IA personnel Changes in senior management	Principal kinds of change	
Change increases risk Change to markets Changes in scope of IA Changes in structure of IA Need for information	Effects of specific changes	
Changing systems Compliance a line management responsibility Focus on business risk	Effects of endemic change	Speed of response Extent of use of risk-based methods
Due diligence Need to find out what acquired Need to integrate systems	Acquisitions	Extent of IA involvement in process integration Extent of IA involvement in risk assessment of acquisition
Need to set up IA department Need to set up corporate governance arrangements	Demerger	Extent of implementation of risk management

Grid 18 Change: acquisitions and demergers		
Concepts	Categories	Dimensions and Properties
Increased complexity Increased costs	Impact of acquisitions	
Integrate acquisitions with group Telling them group policies	Integrating acquisitions	Extent of IA involvement
Finding out what needs doing Finding out what has been acquired	Finding out about the acquisition	Extent of IA involvement
Focusing on core activities Reduction in staff	Impact of demerger on IA of remaining group	Focusing of activities
Starting from scratch New managers/staff	Impact of demerger on IA of demerged group	Influence on organisation and role of IA and on corporate governance

Grid 19 Change: compliance and review		
Concepts	Categories	Dimensions and Properties
Tick and bash Box tick Core compliance work Something needs to be done in the areas which have become unfashionable Sometimes we do a proper audit as well as kick tyres Very rarely a top level risk	Compliance auditing	Extent of compliance auditing
Compliance a management responsibility IA checks processes are working Closer to strategy than compliance Somebody's got to do it – not IA	Responsibility for monitoring compliance	Management responsibility *vs* IA responsibility
Do reviews as well as audits Reviews as opposed to audits Added value as process review	Reviewing	Evidence based *vs* non-evidence based